Steps to  God

A

Correna R. Barzey

Scripture taken from the King James Version of the Bible.

WestBow Press books may be ordered through booksellers or by contacting:

WestBow Press
A Division of Thomas Nelson & Zondervan
1663 Liberty Drive
Bloomington, IN 47403
www.westbowpress.com
1 (866) 928-1240

ISBN: 978-1-9736-2138-6 (sc)
ISBN: 978-1-9736-2139-3 (hc)
ISBN: 978-1-9736-2140-9 (e)

Library of Congress Control Number: 2018902411

Print information available on the last page.

WestBow Press rev. date: 02/27/2018

Acknowledgments

I began writing this book in November 2011 for my children's future reference in helping them to have a better understanding of Jesus Christ. However in the process, the Holy Spirit told me, instead of just for my children, I was to write it so the whole world could read and experience God for themselves. From that point onward, I dedicated myself to this book as it became my passion, purpose, and desire in the hopes of winning souls for Christ and building up His kingdom.

First, I am thankful to God for His help and guidance in the writing of this book. I couldn't have done it without His ever presence in my life, and he is deserving of all the praise and glory.

I also want to thank my children, who were my cheerleaders and gave me quiet time to work on this book. I can't forget my sister and friend, Monica Jeffers-Simon, for always being there.

Finally I would like to thank two wonderful men of God who gave me words of encouragement and hinted that I was on to something great, Pastor Calvin Mills and Bishop Ishmael Charles. A special thanks to Bishop Charles for giving my mini manuscript to Professor David Kinnon to review, who then gave me his honest assessment, for which I am very grateful.

Contents

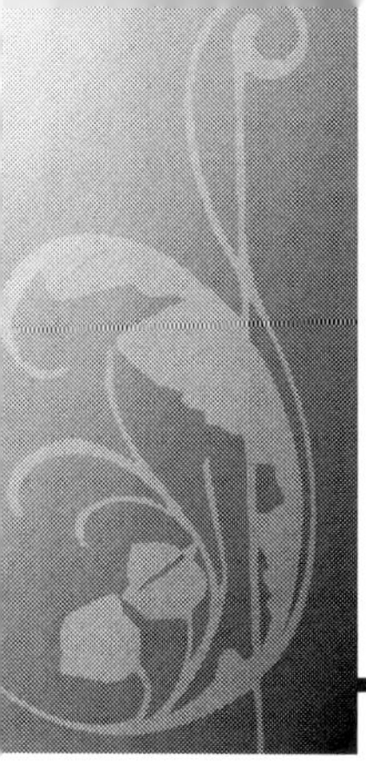

Life with God

A life with God is the most important thing in our life. We have a life that has meaning, fulfillment, and joy. A meaningful life makes a difference not only to us but others in our midst as we shine the love of Christ in this sinful and hopeless world. We know that, wherever our journey takes us, we can rest assured that God is with us and he'll never leaves us or forsake His own. We have full confidence in the God we serve, rejoicing in our present situation, whether good or bad, to the furthering progress of the gospel.

We recognize that our life is not our own. God has a meaningful purpose. It is in the sight of God because he has great and marvelous plans for all mankind, but only if we allow Him to be complete ruler of our lives, thereby putting all our trust and hope in Him as he develops His purpose and will for His glory (1 Cor. 6:19–20).

The key component to having a meaningful and productive life with God is to allow Christ to live His life in and through us, as we are obedient to His Word and fear Him as we develop a relationship with Him. It is imperative that we obey Him and be receptive to His voice as he leads and direct us, so we can experience His presence, wisdom, and strength in all aspects of life, thus growing in godliness. Developing His righteous character, becoming more like Him by demonstrating His love, goodness, and kindness toward others, this shines His light in us living not of the flesh, but instead living by our faith and dependence on God, whereby we receive all of His blessings and favor. As we fear Him and hope in His mercies in our worship and giving Him praise, we recognize that he is a great and powerful God who stands only for righteousness. As a result, we know he will hold each and every one of us accountable for our actions.

A life with God is solely based on our relationship with Jesus Christ, for in Him is filled with all treasures. We must explore and experience this for ourselves in order to develop spiritually and begin a new life with God. Being completely adherent and submissive to the truth of His Word that Jesus Christ is the Son of God, the Savior of the world. Consequently, we receive His grace, love, adoption, learning His ways, and apply those principles into our daily lives. Desiring to do the will he purposed in our life through our actions, attitude, and determination, working only to please Him. Representing Jesus Christ with boldness and courage that brings us hope, joy, and excitement as we focus on God's future rewards awaiting us in heaven, the goal of every Christian. Striving much harder in our works and all we do, for God is faithful to all His promises toward us (Matt. 5:12).

A life with God is having a life that is reconciled to Him. We receive Him into our lives, trusting in Him as our personal Lord and Savior. Having a right standing or relationship with God by our obedience to His commands. Our spiritual life and appetite will be built up stronger in the things of God, whereby our hatred toward sin will be demonstrated by the way we live our lives as we continue with Christ. We make every effort to sin no more, by allowing our love and devotion towards God to manifest itself through our lives to greatly impact those who are in our surroundings. Recognizing that we all human, created equally in the sight of God—no matter our financial status, color, and notoriety—for God places no one above each other, therefore he shows no partiality.

As followers of Christ, motivated in the things of God, we find quality time to spend with Him through our prayers, studying the Word and fellowship with other believers. We realize the meaning of trusting and depending on God as we continually open our hearts, express and surrender our all to Him, consequently receiving His unconditional love and merited favor, experiencing His comfort and goodness. Being rest assured that we are always in His care as he gives us the reassurance and security we need in knowing that he is God. He never goes back on His Word, for the scripture tells, "God says what he mean and mean what he says."

God is happy when our faith and confidence in Him is strong, in return, he blesses us immensely. Knowing this, it propels us to be more spiritual minded, being led by the spirit of God, so the flesh has no power to make us sin against Him. By virtue, we are in oneness with Him (Is. 55:11).

As we continue to live with Christ as the object of our faith, we have full access to Him through His Son Jesus Christ. Having the freedom to approach God with immense confidence, for when he looks at us, he sees the blood of His Son Jesus Christ. We now become a part of the family of God. Exchanging our sin nature, our imperfections for His righteousness, we are welcoming in His presence in our lives. Our bodies become His temple where the Holy Spirit of Christ dwells, thereby edifying and enriching our lives. Procuring the peace of God in our hearts and know certainly that nothing will separate us from obtaining the peace and love of God, "neither death, life nor things present or yet to come" as we remain grounded in Him. Thus building our lives with God in genuine love, faith, and obedience to Him pursuing holiness and righteousness while keeping our eyes fixed on Christ, the author and finisher of our faith (Heb. 12:2).

True followers of Christ are blessed beyond measure. Displaying the radiance, splendor, and everlasting goodness of God, which is the hope of glory, prompting us to share the gospel to others and imparting the love of God in their lives. By doing this, they too can experience the hope and joy, which is available to all who believe in Jesus Christ as saviour.

Having our lives blessed by God, he is in authority over all our well-being, we enjoy the extent of His provision and goodness, exhibiting love for one another by helping those who are less fortunate. Above all, we must love the Lord with all our hearts, minds, and souls, following him at all cost no matter what, denying our own desires and pursuing the things pertaining to Christ and godly living.

Establishing a relationship with God, whereby he knows us and we know Him personally through our constant communication in prayer as he listens to us and we, in turn, worship and obey Him. His power strengthens; therefore participating in the will that he set out for us, becoming a victorious and purposeful follower of Christ.

Jesus came to earth to serve, and we His followers living in Christ, ought to demonstrate the same qualities of service telling others about salvation, the essence of the work of Christ here on this earth. This also gives our lives meaning and a satisfaction while we labor in doing the work of God, pressing forward and winning souls for His glory.

Life with God produces spiritual stability, living in a manner worthy of Him in our every good work. Filled with the knowledge of His will in all spiritual wisdom and understanding, being under the power and direction of the Holy Spirit. Therefore, our behavior must demonstrate that of love, our attitudes and commitments engulfed with love for Christ being devoted to reading and studying His Word.

As we worship the true and living God with adoration and praise, the source of our strength, as we pour out all our earnest devotion to Him, we respect and give love to others by showing humility in all our doing. Holding honest integrity of ourselves giving our resources to the work and ministry of God whether monetary or giving of time, allowing the teachings of God's Word to guide our lives in whatever we do so we can live in holiness and in a right standing with God (Col. 1:10–12).

Living with God is loving Him as we having that deep love and connection with Him, which propels us to want to be more like Him. Therefore, we never waver in our pursuit of holiness and sharing the gospel with everyone who will listen. Fulfilling the Great Commission, the reason why God left us here on this earth, to be His representative and to make disciples of men.

A life with God is something that everyone should look forward to living, having the motivation and a desire of one day seeing Him face-to-face, hearing Him say, "Well done, thou good and faithful servant." A life of meaning is doing something that not only builds up the kingdom of God but shows that God is real, true, and faithful to those who believe and trust in Him as their personal Savior. It illustrates we're doing something that will not only benefit us but others likewise in their future life with God, saving them from the destruction that is yet to come.

Thus, we go forward with God confident in our relationship with Him through His grace, mercy and knowing the truth of Him. Building a strong foundation in Him as we move forward in our faith, as our minds are now renewed with the things of God more and more everyday. Enjoying our relationship with Him, experiencing all of His blessings and spiritual riches that is found in Him. We also receive the glory of God being in complete unity with Him through Christ Jesus. So the world can see the difference in us, thereby bringing glorification and honor to the true and living God.

A life with God is a life without ending; it continues on to eternity.

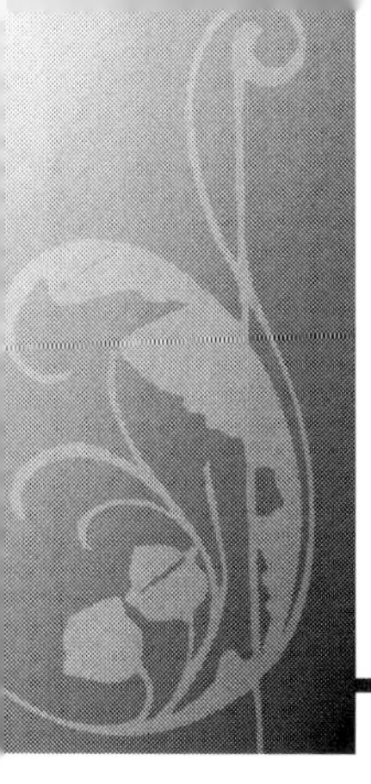

The Power of God's Word

In the Bible, we find the living Word of God, which is God-inspired, it was God-breathed, it comes directly from God as he speak to the hearts of mankind. The Word of God is inerrant and authoritative, for it is profitable for teaching, reproof, correction, and training in righteousness. It is His intention that everyone would know Him through His Word and be guided by His Holy Spirit of Christ. The Bible is the perfect revelation of God Himself, and every word in the Bible is true. The apostle Peter authenticated the Word when he said, "Every prophecies come not by the will of man, but by God as they were moved by the Holy Ghost." The Bible is God's complete revelation to us, which has everything we need to know how to live a life of substance and integrity, providing the necessary guidelines for the road map of our everyday existence (2 Tim. 3:16–17; 2 Peter 1:21).

The Word of God declares His position explicitly and implicitly that it comes directly from God, for it was written over 1600 years ago and remains as one book bound together by historical events, prophecies, fulfillment, and the exaltation of God and His Son Jesus Christ the Messiah. In the Bible, hundreds of times, we see words declaring, "Thus says the Lord or God said," a direct indication that God was speaking to Old Testament Prophets. The apostles Paul and Peter both indicated that the word which they spoke was from God and not from man. The Word of God is unique. It has worldwide appeal. It is spread throughout the world. It produces positive results and is constantly growing and bearing new fruits. This is known as The Gospel of Good News, it cuts away our infected thoughts of committing sin, thereby bringing healing and newness of life to our dying souls. The Word of God lives and remains forever through the Holy Spirit, which is Jesus Christ,"the Word of Life." The Word of God has power that affects lives. It cannot be changed and will never be canceled or rendered void for it is spirit-filled and full of life, accomplishing great things to those who receive it and condemnation to those who reject it (Jer. 11:1–3).

The Word of God always tells the truth. It is God's final word to us. Thus it teaches mankind the values of God, which is good for the soul. It does miraculous works in the lives and hearts of mankind. It also allows us to appreciate the holiness of Christ as it reflects the qualities and characteristics of God, helping us to relate and understand His impact in our lives.

The Bible is without error and mistakes. It's a complete revelation of God, for he is not human. Thus he cannot lie. It is without time, and it will never pass away. It is eternally binding. It is alive, and is active, always doing something to anyone who reads or listens to it. Full of energy, with power to penetrate the hardest of any human heart convicting him or her of their sins, and freeing them from all guilt and shame. Nothing can be hidden from the Word. Once the Word of God is indwelling in your life, it makes a division of the soul and the spirit, and it judges the thoughts and intentions of the heart of mankind, thereby directing them on the right path of life (Num. 23:19; Luke 21:33).

The Word that God gave to us was built upon His grace, wherein Jesus paid the ultimate penalty for all our sins on the cross, demonstrating its power to save, freeing us from the bondage of sin, and setting us apart so we can be nearer to God. It guides and gives us the direction we need to do God's will, helping every true believer to grow in their faith, patterning their lives after Jesus Christ. Becoming firmly rooted in the Word of God and thereby generating strong faith and belief in Christ. Having love for one another and a hoping for the future glory of God. Although our circumstances, people, and things may change, we are certain that the Word of God remains the same, a consistent reminder that the Word of God cannot and will not change, which gives us reassurance and the peace of God that surpasses all understanding (John 17:17, 8:32).

The Word of God communicate to us the reality of Jesus Christ's death and resurrection and the sacrifice he made for mankind, thus persuading us to trust in Christ. As a result, the power of the Word leads us to salvation by our faith and belief in Christ, as we accept Christ into our hearts. The Word then become our guide as how to live a righteous life guiding our steps through life, thus the palmist David says, "Thy word is a lamp unto my feet and a light unto my path."

Therefore, we hold on to its precepts in all situations, as it warns us of consequences and is a great protector by helping us distinguish what is right or wrong, thereby turning us away for our sinful nature. The Word of God "makes wise the simple." As it's a representation of God's wisdom which is imparted in us, assisting us in making wise and prudent decisions in life. The Word is the power source that gives us eternal joy, for we regard it as precious in our eyes as it illuminates God's light, enlightening us for living righteously in the fear of God. (Rom. 1:16; Ps. 119:105).

The Word of God is not just to be read or studied. It is to pierce through the hearts of mankind, hence transforming our lives into that of Jesus Christ. Cutting away our sinful flesh infected by our thoughts and motives, consequently bringing healing and transformation, giving each and every one of us the light of Christ and direction throughout our lives.

One benefit of allowing the Word of God to be a part of your life is that it produces spiritual growth, conducting our lives in a godly manner. It is also a deterrent from sin, allowing us to know God, which in turn gives us the freedom to experience God's richest blessing. In having the Word of God in our hearts, we are proclaiming the gospel of truth, thereby teaching it in the power of the Holy Spirit. We make deep convictions in the heart of mankind and those who believe would live their lives as models of righteousness and holiness (Ps. 119:105, Phil. 2:15).

Through and by the Word of God, we His true followers receive the nutrients which allows our spiritual nature to grow, mature, and bring forth new fruits. The more you know it, read it, and meditate on the Word, the more blessed you become to be a blessing to those who are in your midst. Sin can rob us from God's greatest blessing; therefore we must use the necessary tools he provided for us in His Word, which will liberate us so we can experience God's best in our lives. However, by knowing the Word, it gives us the strength and ability needed to say no to sin and Satan, for God's Word tells us that Satan only comes into our lives to steal, kill and destroy us. Therefore, arming ourselves with the Word of God is vital for our everyday existence. It is like a two-edged sword used to withstand Satan's attacks, and the only weapon we need to fight the war of sin (Eph. 6:17).

For anyone to have a life of stability, productivity, and consistency, it can only be achieved by allowing the Word of Christ to enrich and dwell within them, not just to be reading and studying. Instead, we must learn it by listening, memorizing, knowing it by heart, and following it decisively. The spirit of God and His Word works together to reveal God's will in our lives so we can be conformed into His image, thereby giving us the strength for a spiritual and meaningful life. The Word of God is the authoritative source for living godly. It also gives us God's precepts, His commandments and rule that governs and sustains us in our Christian walk. Having our thoughts and steps align with God in order to survive in this chaotic world.

God's Word is His voice; however, it does not tell us His whole plan for our lives. It just gives us the guidance needed to take the next step toward a purposeful and fulfilling life in Christ. Therefore as His followers, we ought to be attentive to His Word, one of the best and easiest ways of getting to know His plans and purposes for our lives, through the preached Word either on audio or television. Reading and understanding the Word is vital in every believer's life. Hungering for more of His Word, desiring to know Him on a more intimate level. This can only be found though His Word, the way God reveals Himself to us clearly and individually. As we thrive to know Him though His Word in an intimate way, it's important to have a Bible translation to translate the Word along with the help of our Pastors and fellow followers of Christ to get a greater understanding of His Word.

The Word of God confirms and attests to His sovereignty and faithfulness to accomplish that which he has set out to do. Thus, God said, "His words will not return to Him void." It will bring eternal life to those who believe it or judgment to those who reject it. It is the antidote or medicine for the soul, which brings healing clarity in our life and allows it to cleanse and purify our heart, thereby making it new. It creates a life marked by stability, productivity, and consistency, when we allow the Word of God to richly dwell within us. (Is. 55:11; Heb. 4:12).

We gain great wisdom from the Word; we begin to have a spiritual-filled mind as we now have better understanding of the things of God being able to discern both good and evil, the ultimate indication of growth in the truth of God as given in the Word as our guide. This Word is the key to our happiness realizing our self-worth in God. It is the channel where God reveals Himself in us as partakers of Him, as we communicate the truth of His Word to others so they too can acquire and maximize their knowledge of God through His Holy Word.

The Word of God must be our ultimate guide to all truth, the instrument that equips us in what we believe. Most of all, it must be loved and treasured. We hide it in the innermost part of our hearts and minds, as it is the message of truth and the living Word of God. Displaying all the characteristics of God, it is perfect, sure, right, pure, clean, complete, everlasting, and most of all, true. It is divinely inspired as the apostle Paul wrote, "All scriptures is given by inspiration of God, and is profitable for doctrine, for reproof, for correction and for instruction in righteousness." The Word of God reveals His attributes, holiness, sovereignty, righteousness, mercies, kindness, and faithfulness. Therefore it must be received, believed, and obeyed as the final authority in all things pertaining to this life, equipping us for every good work in Christ Jesus. (2 Tim. 3:16).

King David's dominance in battle was because he knew and understood the power of God's Word, and the Holy Spirit was with him. Hence he said, "The spirit of the Lord spake by me and His words was in my tongue," the Word was David's divine inspiration. King David followed God's Word, and he was victorious in battles against his enemies. He never went into a battle without first seeking God in prayer, through which God answered and directed his steps as he battled. He depended on God in every aspect of his life, as evident in many of his Psalms, for he listened and understood God's Word and followed His instructions. King David prepared his heart to be used by God, and thus he was successful and known as a friend of God.

King David emphasized on the power of God's Word as he focused on the creation of this world, which God spoke into existence, "by the Word of the Lord were the heavens made and all the host of them by the breath of His mouth." The Holy Spirit was on King David all his life. For he listened and obeyed the Word of God. His confidence was always built up in God's Word, his secret weapon he needed to go out and fight his enemies, as he always went out in the power and strength of God.

King David feared God. He relied on Him greatly, this fear restrained him from sinning, as demonstrated when he had the opportunity to kill King Saul twice. He knew that God anointed Saul, and as the future king in waiting, God spoke these words to him, "he that rule over men must be just, ruling in the fear of God" (2 Sam. 23:2–3).

David was anointed as king at the tender age of sixteen, and he knew the importance of God's Word and recognized that it had the power to change lives. He obeyed and followed it, today he is known as A Mighty Man of God and a man after God's own heart. He had absolute faith in God, he trusted, depended, and obeyed Him for he loved God. As he often mentioned in his writing of the Psalms, King David had an earnest desire for God as he delight himself in God's Word. He realized that true wisdom only comes from the Word; as a result, he meditated on it day and night. The Word of God was his only source, and he loved it with all his heart, seeking only to do God's will, he allowed the Word of God to indwell him, making it a part of his every existence of life, becoming one with it (Ps. 119:47–78, 37:7).

Our mind is the key to becoming a true follower of Jesus Christ. By this way, we are capable to respond to God's Word by embracing and delighting in His truth and believing by faith in His Word. As followers of Christ, we are the sheep of His pastures, leading us through the paths of righteousness. The more we spend quality time in the Word of God, only then would we be able to experience His love, His protection, and His guidance restoring the right spirit in us. The Word of God brings repentance thus leading mankind into all truth, focusing our minds on the things of God, being aligned and directed by God.

Knowing the Word of God is essential on how we communicate with God in our prayer. Aligning our prayers with the teachings of His Word, thereby refocusing our life on things eternal instead of earthly. The more we know the Word of God, it becomes valuable and precious than any earthly treasures, the psalmist King David says, "They shall be like a tree planted by the rivers of water, that brings forth his fruit in his season; and whatsoever they do shall prosper." The Word of God remains firm in heaven, imparting new life, releasing grace for growth in the faith to live life abundantly with God through His Son Jesus Christ (Ps. 1:2–3).

God's Word is designed to guide, bless, and change lives.

The Uniqueness of the Holy Spirit

The Holy Spirit is the third part of the Blessed Trinity, an expression of God. It is the personal presence of Jesus Christ in that he existed in the beginning of creation and he is also omniscient, omnipotent, and omnipresent. The indwelling of the Holy Spirit is given at salvation to those who believe by faith, an identification of our future glorification of Christ, which is unique and universal. The Holy Spirit is the first work of grace and the first blessing. It bears witness of Jesus Christ and reveals God's truth to the hearts of man. It is known as, the Spirit of Truth, The Comforter, and the Holy Ghost. Most importantly, the Holy Spirit is holy, representing the holiness of Christ. It testifies and glorifies Jesus Christ. It is responsible for our salvation, which places us into the body of Christ, whereby we become partakers and Heirs of God. The Holy Spirit helps us to be obedient, faithful to God and to be appreciative of our newness in Christ, gaining spiritual wisdom to discern the truth, and bearing witness of the truth of Jesus Christ (John 14:16).

The Holy Spirit has many purposes and performs several functions in the body of Christ, accordingly Jesus Christ sent the Holy Spirit to us to help us carry out His mandate. First, the Holy Spirit applies the truth of God's Word in the consciences/minds of mankind to persuade them of their need of the eternal Savior.

Second, the Holy Spirit seals and confirms our eternal status as children of God, thereby becoming our comforter and guide encouraging and exhorting us in our faith as he guides us into the truth of the gospel of Christ. Opening our understanding to receive the revelation of Christ.

Third, the Holy Spirit enriches believers to produce the fruits of the spirit, which develops us into the righteousness of God, as we emulate the characteristics of God. Leading us into spiritual things, pertaining to God and holiness, the Holy Spirit is also the giver of spiritual gifts which enables us believers to be true ambassadors of Christ, showing the grace and glory of God in this world (John 15:26, 16:3).

The Holy Spirit of God is a free gift given to everyone who accepts Jesus Christ because of His love for us. It subconsciously and consciously influences us, thereby bringing us to faith in Christ. We experience His power and personal fellowship with Jesus. The gift of the holy spirit is a one-time occurrence. It is an experience that we receive from God as we accept Him as saviour, thus changing and transforming the life of everyone who believes in Jesus Christ as their personal Lord and Savior. The Holy Spirit acts as a teacher, revealing God's truth to us, living inside us helping us produce godly characters in our lives. Empowering us to perform our ministerial duties. Growing spiritually wise in the things of God as he manifests the holy attributes in the life of the believer. It is a constant companion in our walk of faith, counseling and encouraging us in every aspect of life, exalting Jesus empowering and guiding our lives. The Holy Spirit leads us, gives wisdom on how to live as we thread through the rocky paths of life, as we are not ordinary citizens of this world, but are powerful vessels of God.

The Holy Spirit brings us into a closer and more intimate relationship with Jesus, giving us spiritual wisdom and understanding to accomplish that which he sets out for us, making His power available, strengthening us in our journey. It's our helper, who before God intercedes our prayers on our behalf, giving us the motivation to pray and study the Word, making us aware of our need of His presence and genuine fellowship with Christ. In having the Holy Spirit filling our hearts with love for Christ, we become energized with His Word as His power is manifested greatly through us establishing His presence in our hearts. As the Holy Spirit continually resides within our hearts, we are motivated to live a life based on holiness, remaining steadfast to the Holy Spirit operating and teaching sound doctrines, but most of all it keeps watch over our spiritual life and guarding the faith (Eph. 3:16–19).

One of the main purpose of the Holy Spirit is to convict mankind of their sins, bearing witness of the saving power of Jesus Christ and effecting holiness, thereby creating new believers in Christ. It convicts the consciences of mankind so they can recognize the sins in their lives and the need for God's forgiveness, which will lead them to true repentance, an inward transformation, that will be manifested by our outward actions.

The power of the Holy Spirit is activated into the hearts of believers, freeing us from sin as we commit to God by obeying His Word and fulfilling His purpose here on earth, just as Jesus Himself, who was empowered and anointed with the Holy Spirit, and was able to defeat sin. As the Holy Spirit now resides within us, he leads us and transforms us into the likeness of Jesus Christ, guiding us believers in all truth and expose untruth that may creep into our lives (Rom. 12:2).

Having the Holy Spirit indwell us always, who is Christ's presence, power, and authority it enforces righteousness and truth, that ultimately glorifies God through our constant dedication to Him. We dedicate our bodies as an instrument, a vessel in which God can use for His glory, in the hopes of producing godly fruits for His kingdom. Giving us a deeper understanding of the truth which is found in Jesus, giving clear discernment of the Word of God, changing our minds and thoughts to that of Jesus Christ. As a result of His presence, we are aware of our closeness to Him and the reality of His love, we cautious not to grieve the Holy Spirit. But we instead pursue for His righteousness, striving for a life that brings glory to God. The Holy Spirit gives us the desire to please God, equipping us with the power to accomplish His purpose, having godly desires that only comes out of a heart that is spiritually inclined to God, a person who has an intimate and sincere relationship with Him (John 16:13).

The Holy Spirit testifies of the truth of God. Thereby we can worship the Lord in spirit and in truth, love, and devotion, thereby becoming filled with the Holy Spirit. To be filled with the Holy Spirit, we ought to be obedient, spiritually yielding to God and spiritually mature with knowledge and understanding of His Word, giving the Holy Spirit full control of our lives as he diligently works in and through us.

Being filled with the Holy Spirit is not a one-time time occasion as the indwelling of the spirit upon receiving Christ. Instead it is a repeat experience that occurs at different times, as is evident in the lives of the apostles Paul and Peter. Being filled with the Spirit of Christ, we are careful not to grieve the spirit by remaining true and loyal to Christ and sin not. However, if we sin as followers of Christ, we immediately confess our sins to Him. Jesus was God being conceived by the Holy Spirit and born of a woman. He was also filled with the Holy Ghost from the womb, he came in the form of man yet he lived His life without sin (Acts 4:8, 7:55).

It is God's intentions that we be filled with the Holy Spirit, as he commanded us to be filled with the Spirit. Living by His power to withstand the attacks of the Devil so we can be a testimony to others teaching and strengthening them in the truths of God on how to be victorious over sin. As we continually remain filled with the Holy Spirit of God, we must grow to a level of maturity, which brings us on the path of righteousness, where no longer depend on the flesh (Eph. 5:18).

Being filled with the Holy Spirit of God is not just our outward actions. It deals with our inward thoughts, giving us a mind like Christ, always ready to listen and be obedient to His directives, hence, strengthening His power within us. As the Holy Spirit constantly fills us, it makes real the personal presence of Jesus Christ in us, creating solid confidence within and in our relationship with Him. We not only are in a newness of life, but we are also His children, whereby he gives us spiritual gifts and tools equipping us to serve and be of service for Him.

As the Holy Spirit fills us, we receive spiritual gifts that are supernatural manifestations of the Holy Spirit to strengthen us and others, in particular speaking in tongues which is a sign that a person has the leading of the Holy Spirit and prophesying, which is to declare divine revelation from God to mankind. However, in regard to speaking in tongues, the apostle Paul says, "If any man speak in any unknown tongue, let it be by two or three and that by course and let **one interpret**."

When an individual prophesies a word in the name of Christ, it should come directly from God, therefore we must be vigilant of that which was prophesied. For if it did not come to pass, then you would know it was not under the leading of the Holy Spirit. We as believers in Christ must be able to discern the truth and be aware because Satan has workers who disguise themselves as servants of Christ. Therefore, we ought to test their spirit to see if they are really of God (Acts 14:2:4; 1 John 4:1).

To remain filled with the Holy Spirit, it is important for us to keep our bodies pure as it becomes the temple of the Holy Spirit. It is no longer our own, as such we are careful not to defile it with any immoral or sinful act. Otherwise it would not be able to operate, for the Spirit can only dwell in true believers whose hearts are pure and clean.

Although mankind might be able to fool others, they cannot fool God because he knows the hearts and minds of all mankind. Hence nothing is hidden, if there is no real obedience to God, the Holy Spirit would not be present in our lives. Therefore we all must live by faith, being sanctified to Christ manifesting the fruits of the Spirit as we continue to live in unity with Christ, filled with the acts of worshiping making melody unto God (1 Cor. 3:17).

In the Bible, we learn that John the Baptiste was filled with the Holy Spirit. He too, like Jesus was filled with the Spirit while in their mother's womb. He manifested the Spirit throughout his life and ministry on earth. John was the forerunner for Jesus Christ, preaching and teaching the gospel of repentance and baptizing people in the name of the Lord. Thus he was regarded as a righteous man of God. John was never baptized with the Holy Spirit because the death and resurrection of Jesus Christ had not taken place yet. Hence, Jesus speaks highly of John the Baptiste when he said, "Among those who are born of women there is not a greater prophet than John the Baptiste" (Luke 1:15–25, 7:28).

Jesus told His disciples, "John baptize you with water, but I will baptize you with the Holy Spirit," on the day of Pentecost they received the filling of the Holy Spirit, this identifies believers with the death and resurrection of Jesus Christ, thereby joining us together in the body of Christ.

Baptism of the Holy Spirit is supernatural powers from Christ to us His followers, to empower us for service and witness, accompanying with miracles to proclaim Jesus Christ. Not only does the baptism of the Holy Spirit give us power, it also increases our effectiveness to teach and witness for Christ, for it deepens our relationship with Him, which comes from us being continually filled with the Spirit (Acts 1:5,2:1–4,4,7–8).

Although Jesus was a young boy, he had great wisdom and understanding as he spoke in the temple, the people were all amazed of His great wisdom, for God was with Him. John the Baptiste baptized Jesus in the River Jordan after which he received the baptism of the Holy Spirit as it descended from heaven upon Him in the form of a dove, and the voice of God the Father from heaven said, "Thou art my beloved son; in thee I am well pleased."

Jesus being baptize with the Holy Spirit was anointed and equipped for services to God, and henceforth His ministry began, he received power and authority as he went out performing miraculous miracles. Jesus acknowledge the Holy Spirit upon His life when he said, "The spirit of the Lord is upon me, he has anointed me to preach the gospel to the poor to heal the broken heart, preach deliverance, heal and to preach the acceptance year of the Lord" (Luke 4:18).

The disciples of Jesus ministries did not begin until they received the baptism of the Holy Spirit, which Jesus promised would occur ten days after His ascension back to heaven which took place on the day of Pentecost. After which the disciples ministered with power and boldness, performing supernatural miracles.

This is evident to mankind that we cannot witness God's greatness in our own self effectively, unless we first receive the baptism of the Holy Spirit and continually be filled with the Holy Spirit of Christ. The supernatural power of Christ makes provision to help us when challenges occurs, thereby exerting His power in our witness, freeing us from fear. Hence giving us the courage we need to be warriors for Christ as we proclaim the truth of God throughout this world (Acts 4:14).

Sin hinders us from being filled with the Holy Spirit. However, our obedience to God's commands, consistently feeding the Spirit with the Word, bearing fruits, having genuine desires for God, changing lives and presenting ourselves as instruments in which God can use is the way the filling of the Holy Spirit would be maintained. This allows the Holy Spirit to direct us in time of confusion and distress, whereby he can fill, seal, and sanctify us as followers of Christ, leading us to do the right things, always displaying the characteristics of Christ in victory or defeat.

As we allow the Holy Spirit to dwell in us, our witness must always be with grace, courtesy, and faith, compelling and making mankind thirst for the knowledge of the Word of God, eager to learn more and to be with Him.

Having a ministry-focused mind filled with the Holy Spirit of Christ, we minister in boldness and the power of God's salvation as he releases the full power of the Holy Spirit, exposing sin in the lives of mankind and leading them to a saving faith in Christ Jesus. We do nothing of ourselves but only rely only on the Holy Spirit to transform our minds from physical to eternal things, we draw our strength from Christ and follow the leading of the Holy Spirit.

Demonstrating our spiritual gifts in our witnessing which are signs of our growth and maturity in the faith. Our witness empowered us to denounce sin, call the world to repentance and acceptance of the true and living God. Separated from the world, we are solely committed to God at all costs, testifying of His saving grace, His life, His death, and His resurrection (2 Tim. 1:6–7).

The Spirit of God releases the power of God to change lives for His purpose and will.

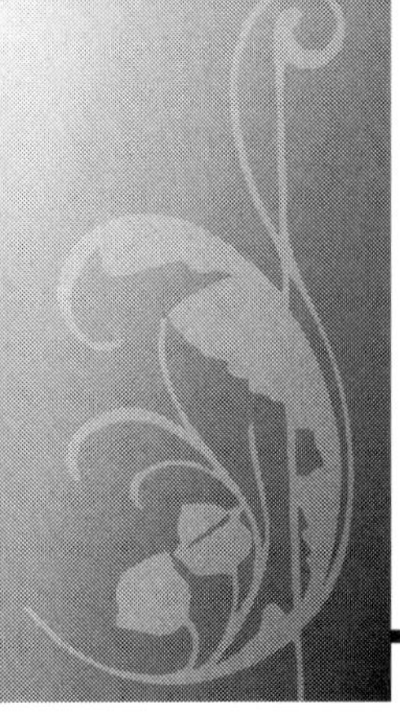

Love of God

God is love, the originator of love, His love is selfless, embracing the whole entire world. He is the first to love us, as he sacrificed His only begotten Son to die on the cross for our sins, which is a true definition of "The Agape Love." God's love is unconditional, eternal, and holy. His mercies, love and graciousness keeps us alive together with Christ Jesus, while providing the source of comfort and calmness needed in this trying world. Conveying a sense of security resting only upon Him, having the assurance that he will protect His own. His nature is that of love, and everything he does flows from His abundant love, which characterizes Him perfectly. He is always true to His nature, and whatever he does comes from His everlasting love, whereby nothing would be able to separate us from His love (1 Cor. 13; 1 John 4:8).

God's love for mankind is freely given, defined by His grace, merited favor, and goodwill, accompanying with His faithfulness and commitment towards us. Even though we are unworthy of His love, he keeps extending it, regardless of our situation even throughout all eternity. His love surpasses all understanding which mankind cannot truly comprehend, for God said, "He have loved us with everlasting love and with loving kindness he draw us." He gave us a life-changing love whereby we find acceptance and love with confidence, knowing that we are His children and he loves us. For His love, provide a plan of redemption and salvation for sinful men. Thus it is immeasurable, unchangeable, and unmistakable, for it is the supreme and dominant attribute of God (Eph. 2:4–5; Jer. 31:3).

Love is the greatest commandment and a powerful thing, the perfect bond of unity and the foundation to understanding God's teachings. It originates in the heart and is essential for obedience to God, as a result of our faith and love for God. A bond of unity, incorporated with our commitment to Christ and each other, the priority of every believer in the body of Christ, being selfless, caring thereby bringing glory unto God. This kind of love is the fundamental practice of our faith in Christ as we grow and mature in Christ. Having the peace of God in of our hearts and obeying His commands to love, "Thou shalt love the Lord thy God with all thy heart and with all thy soul and with all thy mind," and secondly love thy neighbor as thy self (Col. 3:14–15).

Agape Love is God's divine love. Agape Love does not come from human origin. Therefore, for mankind to exhibit such love, it must be a selfless and sacrificial which does not come naturally it must be given out of ourselves. This Agape Love is different from any other love. It's the essence of goodwill and benevolence, and it is a determined act of will that always seeks to benefit others instead of self. To acquire the Agape Love, it can only be produced in our heart through the workings of the Holy Spirit of Christ, upon our acceptance of Christ as His ever presence authenticate what is genuine.

Learning to love one another, modeling our love after Christ and not our own feeling or emotions. Basing our actions and behavior toward others in compassion and not indifference, meeting others' needs, displaying the virtues of God in humility and selflessness basing our love on God as we live a life of love. By being obedient to His command of love, we will be truly bless by it, making perfect love in our hearts and bringing us into the right framework of God (1 John 4:8; Lev. 19:18).

Loving God is a very important aspect in living as Christians. We cannot be a Christians without loving Him, for it shows others that we are His followers and we live for Him and Him through us as we reflect His characters and fullness in our daily life. In order for one to truly love God, first he or she must be obedient to Him for this shows evidence of our love and faithfulness toward Him. As we form an intimate relationship with Him, by loving our neighbors as our self. Only through the transformation of our heart, minds, and soul are we able to love other as God commanded, putting nothing above God and striving to love righteously with compassion and selflessness. In our love for God, we must always demonstrate our loyalty and allegiance to Him, thereby committing ourselves to Him wholeheartedly, growing and standing firm in our faith and all things that pertain to godliness (Matt. 22:37).

To grow in the love of God, we must accept His forgiveness, and only then will we experience His love. Whereby grow in the knowledge of His love by the reading and studying of His Word, loving Him with all our heart, mind, and soul the complete expression of our trust in Him. However, our growth in His love is best seen in our actions toward others, which then will result in our blessings that he bestows on us as we steadfastly love and live in Christ. Therefore, in having full knowledge and recipient of His love, which His Word reveals we are careful not to compromise the supremacy and righteous standards of Christ by always displaying His love every day. God's actions are based on His love. So too should we His followers, demonstrate our love to the world so we may be known as disciples in our actions towards others (John 13:35).

It is important to note that loving ourselves is absolute paramount in order for us to appreciate ourselves and love God and our neighbors as ourselves. Therefore we must accept and embrace everything there is about us, knowing that we are fearfully and wonderfully made in the sight of God. The more we love and appreciate ourselves, the more we will come to the realization of why God placed such value on us to love our neighbors as our self, knowing he created us to be in relationship with Him and others. We are all individually unique in our own way, and we realize the need for God's love so we accept His redemption, which enables us to love and experience His love intimately.

And as we love Him and ourselves, our heart will lead us to be obedient to His commands. We were created in the image of God and are considered worthy and somebody of great value in His eyes. And as followers of Christ, we bear His image in our hearts and minds, living in love, righteousness, and true holiness (Col. 3:10).

We love God because he first loved us. Therefore our love towards God should always involve the affections of our hearts, the center of our emotions, whereby he is highly esteemed. It is an expression of our obedience and actions in our glorification of Him here on earth. Our love is the distinguishing mark as followers of Christ, where the world can see our love based on selflessness. It is a sacrificial love that seeks the good in others, the kind of love Jesus has for His followers, which produces stability in our life. Treating others with kindness, consideration, and respect, being inspired by God's love, displaying His characteristics such as long-suffering, humility, thoughtfulness, forgiveness, and patience, which are all eternally binding and the fruits of the spirit (Gal. 5:22–23).

God's love motivates His compassion and mercy in our hearts, which then brings forth His transformation and love, meeting all the emotional, physical, and spiritual needs in us and to those who we show and give love to, thereby making it easy to manifest it outwardly. True godly love will produce sacrifice in our actions and will be seen by others and ourselves, receiving a sense of great satisfaction for the love that is in our lives. This is the very nature of God. The more you love Him, the more love you have for others, giving us motivation for living a stronger Spirit-filled Christian life. In having great love towards God, only then will all His commands in the Bible begins to make sense as we strive to live in the truth of Word and maintaining unity in the faith.

A deep love for God is necessary for a deep, solid relationship with Him, which produces a life filled with the richness of His glory, and our love for one another by expressing sincerity in helping others in need. Our faith and hope increases more in Christ when we have love in our heart, for it is because God loves us so much that he separated us from the world so we can be an example, the light that shows the love of God and faith in Him, effectively changing lives for the better. God's perfect love is extended to all mankind, and all we have to do is recognize and accept His love which he provided in salvation (1 John 4:7).

Our love for others should not harbor jealousy and envy. It should always work out for the good of others, seeking to provide service to them, honoring God in everything we do, and maintaining unity. Resolving problems and reconciling differences by being loyal to Christ always speaks the truth in love. God values love immensely, therefore our attitude, behavior, and actions defines the quality of our love, whether it be of patience and long-suffering, tolerant to others' feelings, being humble, and always showing the kindness of God. Our love is the manifestation of the spirit of God, desiring to help and bless others, that motivates us, always providing service to encourage and build others up.

The scriptures says, without love, we are nothing in the sight of God.

No matter how many poor and needy people you feed or what spiritual gifts we process, without having love in our heart, it is rendered useless or unprofitable to God. Good work without love does not impress God. Therefore in whatever we do, it must characterize God for it is to be rendered valuable and of purpose to Him. Even if possessing strong faith and hope and no love it is worth nothing to God, God says "love bears, believes, and hopes all things" for love emphasizes who they truly are. Love is a spiritual gift that is expressed in a supernatural way that comes from deep within the heart of God and is extended to us, which when expressed in us, Christ will never fail (1 Cor. 13:1–13).

The greatest person to model our love after is God Himself. He provided His love to mankind in so many ways, which embodies who he truly is. And that is love. He gave His Son Jesus Christ as a ransom for our sins so we could have access to Him and be Heirs of His kingdom through His grace and His mercies. He is a God that does not stay angry forever, and does not always give us the punishment we deserve. All he requires is for us to accept His Son Jesus Christ and be saved. His truth came through Jesus, and this truth shall set all mankind free from the bondage of sin through His love and forgiveness (John 1:17; Ps. 145:8).

God's love is merciful, gracious, and transcending. It lasts throughout eternity for it is an act of giving, and there is no condition to His great love, for it is with us all the time. The Holy Spirit fills our hearts with His love daily. As a result of His love for us, the scriptures says, "Whom the Lord loves he chastise," which is to show us that he cares and we are important to Him. It leads us to repent and restore God's blessings. And to promote holiness, we then continue to live as His spiritual children. We can see His love through history, as he kept providing for the children of Israel in the wilderness for forty years, and also in our lives as he continues to bless and provide for us (Heb. 12:6; Rom. 8:35).

The love of God is always trustworthy for it protects and bears no record of wrongdoing, it is pure, for no selfishness or sin is found in it, and it is sacred.

God entrusts us His followers with His love, which comes with great responsibility as we ought to enrich others with the love of God, motivating their hearts towards a greater goal in life. His love brings liberation and wholeness in the lives of those who are in need of it most, showing us that there is a greater purpose for our existence here on earth, striving towards the higher calling in Christ Jesus. Showing love in everything we do, being an example of what God expects and wants His followers to be, which is a replica of Him. Filling our hearts with His love and the hope of the future glory in Christ Jesus (Rom. 5:5).

Believers in Christ are admonished love without restraints, and conditions, it does not destroy or put others down. Instead, it is a calm exterior that builds up, showing kindness that motivates and directs others in the right direction of life, which leads to righteous living in Christ Jesus. The Word of God says love bears all things, believes all things, hope all things, and endures all things. As we go through our life journey here on earth, let's demonstrate genuine love for God and others with humility and grace (1 Cor. 13:7).

To live for God is to live in love.

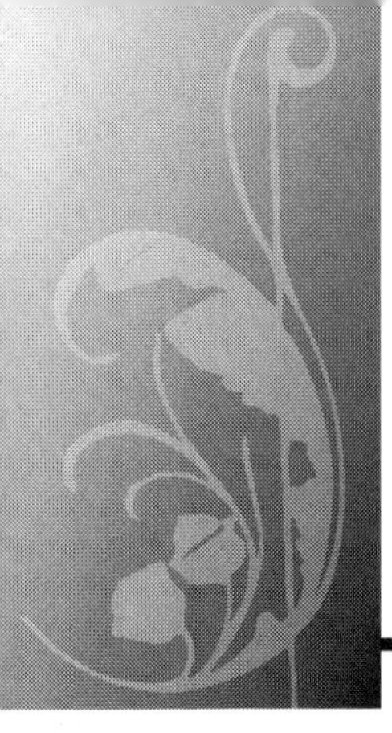

Wisdom of God

God is all wise with infinite wisdom, he is the source of all wisdom. It comes from and through Him. His wisdom is the ultimate and original wisdom, that is from above full of mercy without partiality and hypocrisy. The wisdom of God is eternal, which is evident in His work, His Son Jesus Christ, and His omniscience. In the sovereignty of Him are all the treasures of wisdom and understanding. As the scriptures says, "For he gives wisdom and out of His mouth comes knowledge and understanding, the depth of His wisdom is unsearchable," which is apparent in creation for there is no limit to His wisdom. His wisdom is manifested in His Word, the Holy Scriptures which are recorded in the Bible, and is God-breathed, whereby mankind can learn and be edified on how endless the wisdom he processes (Jer. 51:15; James 3:17).

God's wisdom is a characteristic of who he is, for it is sure and unchanging, pure, and perfect. There is no end to His wisdom for it is extended throughout eternity. Mere mankind cannot comprehend its depths. His wisdom is filled with power, which was clearly visible as Jesus Christ hung on the cross, God dealt with sin by providing a righteous sacrifice for the sin of all mankind, making a way for us to have access to Him through His Son Jesus Christ.

With God, nothing can never be a mystery, His wisdom is unsearchable. It cannot be traced or duplicated for he is the giver of wisdom. He gives to the wise, knowledgeable, and understanding. God is all knowing. In Him are wisdom, might, council, and understanding. His wisdom is far more superior than that of mankind's wisdom.

It is important to know that there are two different types of wisdom:

heavenly wisdom, which is from God, and earthly wisdom, which is from mankind's own wisdom. These two wisdom are distinctively different from each other, one is of God and the other is of Satan (Dan. 2:21–22).

Wisdom begins with the reverence and the fear of God, for the scriptures tells us, "The fear of the Lord is the beginning of wisdom," which prompts us to trust and accept Jesus Christ into our lives, the way mankind can possess and receive the wisdom of God, thereby gaining spiritual knowledge and understanding. His wisdom is free to those who seek it, for the scriptures tells us, "If you lack wisdom let him ask of God," just as King Solomon asked for wisdom and was granted by God. We His followers have the same privilege of asking God for wisdom in prayer by faith while continuing to abide in Him and His words abiding in us. The wisdom of God can only be revealed by the Holy Spirit of God, which gives us knowledge of the revelation of God, opening the eyes of mankind so they can see His power through Jesus Christ crucified (Ps. 111:10, 3:9).

Wisdom is a valuable gift from God. It is better than all the riches in the world and is one of the most important virtues in life where we can speak biblical truths with God's discernment, and applying it to life's situations. To be filled with the wisdom of God, we must be first filled with the Holy Spirit, and asking God in our prayer. The apostle James said in his epistle, "If anyone lack wisdom let him ask of God who gives to all man liberally." Thereby we walk wisely in the light and love, realizing the importance of redeeming the times that the Lord have given us to do His will, having our desires and thoughts on Christ (James 1:5, 3:17).

True godly wisdom is having spiritual capacity to emulate life from God's prospective, thereby making the right choices and decisions, doing things according to His will, through the guidance of the Holy Spirit. The wisdom of God is pure, peaceable, gentle, easy, and full of mercy, it always leads to good results, allowing us to walk safely in God's goodness, and not be trapped or destroyed by the enemy. In obtaining the wisdom of God, we must be adhering to God's Word, being sensitive and mature in the knowledge of God, having the discernment on how to examine and approve God's will as he guides us into the situations of life. This is the ability of finding the principles from God's Word and use the knowledge gained, and applying it into our lives.

God gives wisdom, and from His mouth comes knowledge through discipline. We apply spiritual truths into our lives, as the Holy Spirit allows us to see matters as God sees things so we can speak to the spiritual needs of mankind, resulting in good, bringing honor and glory to God (Isa. 11:1–3).

Wisdom cannot exist without knowledge. They are in conjunction with each other, which leads to a deeper appreciation of God, and using His wisdom and knowledge to edify others. Just as wisdom is a gift from God, so too is knowledge and understanding. He places His laws and rules over our lives as he generously grants to us His knowledge, for he desires us to know Him on an intimate level. Jesus Christ embodies the knowledge of God His Father, and as the scriptures says, "In Jesus Christ are hidden all the treasures of wisdom and knowledge." (Col. 2:2–3).

Wisdom of God is not the amount of education and knowledge a person acquires or has. It is living and thinking according to God's righteousness standards, thus abiding, being obedient, and having a personal relationship with Him through the Holy Spirit. As we grow with God, our knowledge will be pleasant to our souls, producing life and power, knowing that the more time we spend in His Word, the more we understand the difference between the wisdom of the world and the wisdom of God. The knowledge to understand and discern spiritual things, opening our eyes to see what the hope of God brings as we are being established in His favor and grace, relying only on His wisdom, making the necessary changes needed to be in the light of God.

Earthly wisdom believes that there are many ways to God. Seeing is believing, which deals with mankind's emotions, it is not spiritually inclined with God, but instead it's of the Devil and has no real permanent worth because it would be canceled out at death. It is limited and subjected to errors. This earthly wisdom is established on prestige, promotion, the influence of money, and important people in society who makes humanity the highest authority, hence refusing to recognize the revelations of God. They depend solely on their own understanding. Demonstrating their own human spirit, which leads to pride, depending only on their wisdom, self-righteousness, vanity, and the carnal thoughts of the wise. Focusing more on self-sufficiency and self-ambitions, appealing to the senses and emotions, which is based only upon that which can be seen, touched, and heard. Thus the scriptures tells us, "Earthly wisdom is foolishness with God" (1 Cor. 3:19).

Earthly wisdom only pertains to a person's humanness, for scripture says, "The natural man receives not the things the spirit of God and neither can they know the things of God," a natural man only understands natural things, and their solutions are purely humanistic and earthly. The wisdom of the earth has no permanent worth, it opposes the truth of God's Word and leads people away from faith in God, thus it is inadequate to bring anyone to salvation, it places confidence in human leaders and not God. This earthly wisdom would only lead to self-deception, where people believe that they are wise in their own eyes, thereby failing to realize that God is the Creator and giver of wisdom as he knows the thoughts of all mankind. They are vain thoughts that are filled with wickedness and self-flattery and would not endure throughout eternity. It is merely earthbound. Earthly wisdom is restricted having temporal truths, which eventually will lead to disappointments, regrets, and pain because it is only based upon mankind's opinions. Hence, it would not be able to achieve its maximum purpose (1 Cor. 2:14, 3:19–20).

Earthly wisdom is motivated by the devil, earthly principles, and purposes. It's from mankind's own viewpoint that will only serve the things that are earthly; thus it would not be able to withstand the test of time because it is flawed and futile. This earthly wisdom produces confusion, sin, and evil works, for it is self-deceiving as mankind would at every given chance, express its own opinion by displaying its intellectual arrogance, self-sufficiency, and most of all, pride, the core and root of this earthly wisdom.

The world's wisdom is always seeking the approval of mankind, whereby they can achieve and maintain their grounds for boasting of one self, which leads them to be self-centered, believing they are wise and all knowing. This wisdom is the work of the Devil. Thus the Word of God says, "This wisdom is earthly, sensual and devilish," which is secular, unspiritual, and demonic. Simply put, it is like the lust of the flesh. Do what is right in your eyes, that is the wisdom of the Devil (James 3:14–16).

With this earthly wisdom, it would be difficult to find the true purpose of life, it only appeals to mankind's senses and emotions, it is not peaceable and pure. Instead, it demonstrates anger, a decisive spirit, and ungodly attitudes, that would not bring real satisfaction or peace. Earthly wisdom is self-seeking and cares only for itself and the things of this world and its achievements, placing one's feelings in high esteem, allowing themselves to be directed and guided by Satan, which will only result in destruction and deception. Seeking and craving for power, titles, status, and notability eventually leads to jealousy, selfish motives and lustful desires, causing mankind to have no real desire to serve God. As a result, they are lost in God's eyes and he considers them as fools. The wisdom of the earth is basically all about getting what you want in this life, such as power, pleasure, money, fame, and independence, all of which is opposed to the wisdom of God. In having this wisdom, it will not bring peace of mind, happiness, and joy. Instead, it will bring heartache, pain, and a soul being tormented in hellfire throughout eternity.

This earthly wisdom is futile and merely the theory of mankind's fleshly opinion and speculation, which cannot bring lasting solutions to our problems. Nor can it help us understand the heart and mind of God. Earthly wisdom does not consider God as the sovereign ruler over mankind and this world. They are so caught up in themselves that they use being wealthy as an indication of a person's wisdom and knowledge. Mankind cannot find true wisdom because evil ambitions ensnare them. They fail to realize that, and when death comes, all their wisdom and knowledge will perish with them and would render as worthless. However, the excellency of knowledge is the wisdom that gives life when we come to the realization that our intellectual pride and human wisdom is foolishness apart from God (Eccl. 7:23).

King Solomon loved the Lord. He followed the statuses of his father, King David. He asked God for wisdom so he could discern good and evil, which God gave to him, and thus he became the wisest man who ever lived. All the nations marveled and came to hear his wisdom. God also blessed him with great wealth, both in riches and honor; however, God gave him a command along with a promise "to walk in the ways of God, keep His statutes and commandment" of which he must obey and would lengthen his days. King Solomon, with all the wisdom and blessing, still became disobedient to God's command. He stopped pursuing after God and turned his desires to the pleasures of all earthly enjoyment, such as lusting of the flesh. He disobeyed God's commands to the people of Israel "not to marry foreign women" and "not to worship any other God." King Solomon's disobedience led him into worshiping false gods, thereby allowing his desires to rule his heart and instead of God (1 Kings 3:14; Deut. 7:3).

Although Solomon was the wisest man on earth and had the wisdom of God, he still allowed Satan to work his wisdom against him, Solomon gave into his fleshly lust, thus falling into Satan's trap and putting to shame the wisdom that God gave to him. King Solomon's disobedience demonstrated to us that no amount of wisdom can withstand sin if we are not obedient to God and His Word, for we are all flesh. The Bible says "the flesh is weak," King Solomon's heart was turned away from God and he did evil in the sight of God. God gave Solomon the free will to choose right and obey Him, but Solomon chose his own wisdom, that of the world, instead of the wisdom of God. And he fell prey to his prideful and sinful lust. At the end of King Solomon's life, he realized his errors and the great destruction of his disobedience as he reflected on his youthful life. He admonished mankind "to rejoice in our youthful years; and in rejoicing know that God will hold us accountable for our actions." We must acknowledged God from youth and followed Him. For worldly wisdom, pleasures of life, and wealth, all these things really boils down to "are vanity and vexation of the spirit." Instead, we ought to fear God and keep His commandments for that is the duty of all mankind (Eccl. 1:14, 11:9).

There is a limitation to human wisdom and the uncertainty of life under the sun. Only God knows the future. Therefore we must always seek His wisdom along with the guiding of the Holy Spirit in our everyday life. Jesus is the embodiment of God. He is filled with incomprehensible wisdom "all things are from Him, though Him and to Him, there is none wiser." Fear Him, strive in having the mind of Him, lean not onto our own wisdom but onto God's wisdom. King Solomon demonstrated to us how having wisdom and not depending and following God would be detrimental to one's life. Therefore, in gaining God's wisdom, we should apply our hearts to His instructions with a hunger for His knowledge through His Word and prayers. Keep a close relationship with God to be able to discern earthly wisdom apart from God's wisdom, for the wisdom of God will be manifested in our good works, the way we live, and an attitude of meekness (Rom. 11:36; 1 Cor. 2:16).

King Solomon cautioned mankind when he said, "Wisdom under the sun, apart from God is unfulfilled and meaningless," for he could not gain satisfaction to himself, he wanted to please himself instead of God. It's only when God's wisdom enters mankind's hearts that their inward motives, desires, and thoughts produce life and power which keeps us focused on Him, walking in the safety of the good and perfect will of God. To live a meaningful life, which is blessed with the promises of God, we must humble ourselves, and repent. Ask God for His wisdom, setting our minds on things above and not things on this earth to become wise in the things of God.

One day, everything on this earth will all be destroyed. Nothing earthly will last forever. Do not seek earthly wisdom and pleasures of the world for they are all "vanity," when you die, we cannot take anything with us. Therefore, instead of building up your treasures here on earth, why not build up your treasures in heaven by being obedient to God? (Col. 3:2; Eccl. 7:12).

Knowledge comes from God's Word, but wisdom and understanding comes directly from God.

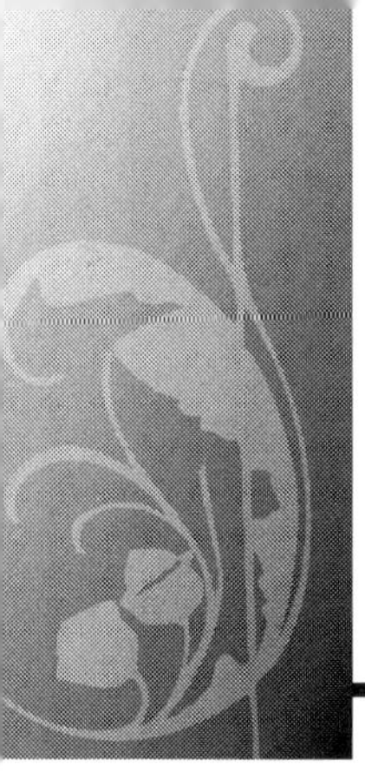

Being Committed to God

Being committed to God begins and ends with understanding and living out God's expectations in our life, making Him sole authority, having total and complete control over our lives. Continually being obedient to His commandments. Commitment to God is allowing Him to be our compass and guiding light while we are His servants here on earth, being faithful and blameless before Him, living according to His Word. It's a life of obedience, believing, trusting diligently, and serving God according to His will. Committing our ways unto Him, putting His will ahead of our own while acknowledging Him in all aspects of our lives. Incorporating God in our plans, decisions, and activities. Desiring to please Him, no matter the consequence; loving the things he loves; and hating the things he hates (Ps. 3:6).

Our commitment to God should be based absolutely on our actions in responding to His Word and commands. Always ready to be totally committed and having genuine fellowship with Him. For it's all about our choices and determination to follow Christ, not being undecided in the faith but being firmly rooted and faithful in all things pertaining to Christ, constantly moving forward with Him, knowing we can and do all things through Christ that strengthens us.

By our genuine commitment to God, it will be validated in our love for Him. Showing Him our gratitude and loyalty as His Word indwells our minds filling us with His grace, which builds up, nourishes, and strengthen us so we can be a blessing to others by leading them to Christ (Deut. 6:5–7; Phil. 4:13).

Our deep love for God, fearing and serving Him in sincerity, truth, and strict obedience to Him, is the component that drives followers of Christ to be totally committed to Him. It constrains and propels us to do service for Him and others in our actions and languages, lifting and exalting His holy name while testifying of His greatness in the process. In our demonstrations of Christ, it's incumbent that we live a life that is blameless, filled with patience, perseverance, and endurance, holding strong in our faith and keeping our eyes on God, the source of our strength. Responding to matters in totality of the truth of God's Word, building up our faith and developing spiritual characters in our continuation in the fight for the gospel of truth. Standing strong and never grow weary (Heb. 12:1–2).

It is imperative to understand that, to be committed totally to God, we must love Him with our whole heart and our entire being, which will then sustain us as we go through troubling times, yielding only to the Holy Spirit of Christ, the most important aspects of us staying committed to Him. Engrossed always in the glory of God, His mercy, grace, wisdom, holiness, and faithfulness. Holding back nothing, placing God in high esteem way above everything. Denying self in our sacrifice and service. Standing by the principles of Christ which is the truth. Safeguarding ourselves from deceptive influences, living in integrity, faith, and complete submission to God's will and directives. Speaking the truth always in every situation for His truth sanctifies and sets us free as he continues to make our crooked paths straight and lead us through with His powerful hands, trusting in His power for he is the all-powerful God (Luke 12:31–35).

In remaining committed to God, our devotion and loyalty to Him is essential. Even under immense pressure, we courageously defend and stand up for Him, no matter the cost, and in all things, never jeopardize our relationship with Him. Instead, we continue to move forward with God, being preoccupied with Jesus. Striving for holiness, modeling our lives after Jesus Christ, who was committed to His Father in all things, even as to dying on the cross for our sins. He is our motivation, our anchor that holds us together, for the scriptures tells us, "We must not be weary in good doing for in due season we will reap if we faint not." Jesus did not give up, even through all His suffering, we too must be strong and vigilant, for he will not give up on us if we remain committed to Him.

He will strengthen us when we are weak, feed us when we hunger, and bc the living water when we thirst so we faint not (Gal. 6:9).

The Bible tells us, "The eyes of the Lord run throughout the entire world to show Himself strong in those whose heart is towards Him." Those who are committed to Him, would experience the manifestation of God's love, His strong support, encouraging us to remain dedicated and committed. In our constant communication with God, by feasting on His Word, praying and fasting, we develop a more intimate connection with Him and our desires to be His disciples. Jesus told His disciples, "If you continue in my word then you are my disciples," which not only shows our commitment to Him, but describes what he desires from His children. God sees the hearts of every mankind, and he knows our level of commitment towards Him. Our hearts, minds, and souls should always work together for the good of God, for we are His servants here on earth to spread the gospel and build others up in the love of Christ (1 Tim. 4:16).

As we remain committed to God in our willingness to stand firm, we uncompromisingly rely completely on His guidance and direction, resting assured that His presence is ever with us in all we do, bringing glorification unto Himself. Henceforth, we do not focus on our present circumstances, but only look to Christ, finishing the race set before us by remaining true to Him, knowing that our rewards awaits us in heaven. Our affect on others' lives will be successful and fruitful in accordance to the plans that God has purposed for us because of our love and obedience to Him. His Word, creates new lives in Christ and one day, we will say like the apostle Paul, "I have fought a good fight, I have finished my race and have kept the faith and there is laid up for me a crown of righteousness which the Lord the righteous judge will give me," This is the goal of all followers of Christ (2 Tim. 4:7–8).

In the Bible, we read the story of the prophet Daniel, a committed and faithful servant of God who loved the Lord with all his heart and soul. His loyalty to God earned him the position of leadership in the godless kingdom of Babylon. He committed himself to God as a youth, and he continued being faithful to God throughout his entire life, thus making his story such a compelling and intriguing life lesson in which believers of Christ can model and live by remaining true to the living God. In every circumstance, Daniel always takes the opportunity to use them for the glorification of God. And with God's help, he continued to stand firm in his convictions and commitment to God. Daniel had an obedient and submissive heart towards God. Despite his challenges and circumstances, he always chose God rather than man, even when his own life was in jeopardy, he remained strong in his faith, bringing glory to God in everything he did (Dan. 1–12).

Daniel was determined to worship and serve God at all costs, and he would not compromise his beliefs or the things of God. Hence he had favor in the eyes of God throughout the three different kings he served under. Daniel continued to grow in the wisdom, knowledge, and understanding of God, for the scriptures says, "He had an excellent spirit," which was the Holy Spirit of God, the dominant factor in his life that kept and strengthened him for which God and mankind held him in high esteem. Daniel also was a man of prayer, purpose, and power, but most importantly, he had great respect and fear for God more than he did for anyone.

He kept his focus only on God, he knew that for his commitment, God would honor his choices of obeying His divine laws and commandments and not surrendering to the commands of the kings. His life was built and centered on God, humility and having a disciplined prayer life, where he would commune daily with God on every situation in his life, having confidence that God was able to deliver him (Dan. 5:12, 6:3,10).

Today, God is looking for Daniels in us, His followers to represent Him with great influence and commitment. Followers who would not be worried about what the people of the world will do to them, but to be genuinely committed to all God's principles and ways. He wants us to be committed to Him, which brings both suffering and rewards in this life, demonstrating our faithfulness, integrity, and humility in our faith, embracing challenges and be faithful laborers of God while persevering until the very end. Creating the spiritual discipline needed to be stable, focused, and poised in the midst of our situations where our faith and godly characters would be built up and not be shaken in trials, as the scriptures says, "He will keep us in perfect peace, whose mind is stayed on Him." For God is the rock who endures forever and the sure and firm foundation on which we can stand victorious, but first, we ought to place our trust and hope in Him (Is. 26:3).

To be genuinely committed to God, we must exhibit full knowledge of His Word and will. Being attentive to the interest of God, not the interest of man. We must be humble, featuring the attitudes of Christ and a life that will influence this world. Continually being strong and courageous in our faith, trusting only in the sovereignty and provision of God, as he guides, protects, and preserves us in all things that pertains to His righteousness. Jesus Christ is the chief example of total commitment to God the Father, and we as His followers must be committed whether in life or death, for we know he will deliver us. In the end, it will be worth it all, for in Christ we live and move, and have our being for we are His children (Acts 17:28).

To be genuinely committed to God is self-denial and cross bearing being crucified with Christ.

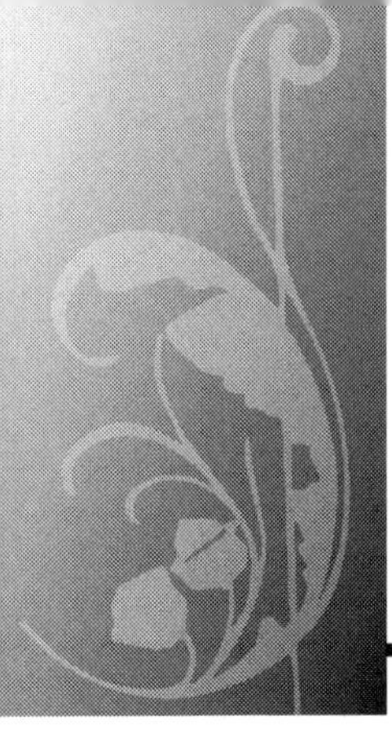

Importance of Prayer

Praying is a biblical principle, and it's a command from God. It is the avenue on how to know God's will for our lives. Prayer is a sign of our obedience to God. It builds up our relationship with Christ and helps us to overcome sins and temptations. Prayer is communicating with Christ in an intimate way where we call and cry out to Him, lifting our souls and seeking the Lord with our whole hearts, desiring fellowship while declaring our dependence on Him, for he alone is in control. It helps us to keep our relationship with God intact whereby we humble ourselves before Him in praise and thanksgiving, drawing us closer as our relationship grows stronger, focus and alert, having our mind stayed on Him. Prayer is sincerely expressing our innermost spiritual thoughts and needs to God, allowing Christ to be in every aspect of our lives, a natural process where we are opening up our heart to Him, the primary channel to God as we hear His voice (Eph. 6:12,18).

Prayer allows us to worship and praise God, offering confession of sins, which leads to genuine repentance. Prayer is an integral element of the Christian faith, one of the nutrients for steadfastness and stability in our everyday walk with Christ. Prayer is connected to our action of faith in Jesus Christ for salvation, believing he will answer our prayers and receiving His grace, and as a result granting us eternal life, thereby becoming a member of the family of Christ and Heirs of the Kingdom of God.

The best way of communing with God is through prayer. It is also important in our daily life, whereby we share all aspects of our life with Him, genuine in our love for Him, sincerity in our hearts, and delighting in His goodness. Reverencing our awesome savior Jesus Christ and submitting to His Lordship, worshiping Him with adoration, which gives us the privilege to gain access to Him, as we continue to have a purposeful and prayerful life (1 Thess. 5:16–18).

God values prayer, His deepest desire for mankind, the ultimate expression of our heart towards Him, which in turn, he treasures our word of praise, petition, and adoration. He desires fellowship with us His followers, in our prayers and fasting, for it brings Him joy, as it is the epic expression of our love and gratitude of His undeniable favor in our life. Our prayers become more vital for wisdom, and understanding of the truth of His Word, whereby we find strength, guidance, and peace, for it is one of the weapons needed to be victorious over sin and to accomplish His work here on earth. Clearing our path of both physical and spiritual obstacles, which may hinders us from completing the plans he has set out for us. Therefore it is imperative we go to God in prayer in all openness, knowing he is the God of creation, grace, deliverance, and revelation and the one who supplies our needs and answers prayers. Being persistent in devoting ourselves to prayer, having a designed time where we can speak to God on a daily basis, another key to a successful Christian walk in all levels of our life.

In all our praying, we must ask God for spiritual understanding and wisdom to discern His will, knowledge, and abundant presences of the Holy Spirit to unlock God's power in our lives. To become more spiritually alert. Becoming both visually and mentally alert to the leading of God, for there is no limitation to the power of prayer when our hearts are lifted up towards Him.

Jesus encouraged His disciples to pray "that they enter not into temptation." The Devil is out to steal and destroy the children of God. Therefore, having a deep prayer life is vital so we can overcome temptation and grow spiritually with God. Praying in the spirit is the spiritual weapon needed to overcome Satan, it's through prayers, faith, and trust in God, that we can be victorious over Satan (Luke 22:40,46).

Prayer is a natural activity for Christians. Our declaration and dependence on God Almighty, forming a unique relationship with Him, as he directs us through our prayers. It's a necessity for our spiritual life, growth, and maturity. It strengthens us for the journey and His will, to receive His favor, and grace to help. Thus we become confident and strong in the faith, knowing he will answer our prayer to accomplish His work, thereby bringing glory to Him in our influences of others.

In our prayer, we must petition the needs of others to help in their circumstances of life, but mostly to help persons find Christ, the greatest gift we can give to another. This selflessness reflects God's character, the outpouring of His love and mercy as we grow in compassion. Through the effectiveness of our prayers and by the power of the Holy Spirit working in and through us, and with great power we can witness to others about the true and living God (Phil. 4:6).

Jesus, who is a part of the Holy Trinity of God, came to earth to be a servant, leaving behind all His heavenly treasures and powers, hence, he needed to be constantly communing with His father. He prayed always to God for revitalization and clarification when making decisions. Jesus was devoted to prayer, and it was the priority of His life and ministry. He prayed to His Father for strength, direction, guidance, and protection and to always be submissive to God's will.

In human form, Jesus prayed to learn obedience to His Father. He also prayed for divine wisdom and power to perform miracles and to overcome temptations. His dependence on prayer was a way of life for Him and His constant communications with His Father. His prayers empowered Him to remain focused for the task ahead, Calvary, to carry out God's plan of the redemption for mankind and to show them that prayer was necessary for righteous living, to do God's will and be victorious in this life and beyond (John 10:30; Heb. 5:8).

It's important to know that God hears all prayers. Nothing goes by Him, he is sovereign. However, he does not answer the prayers of everyone. He only answers the prayers that are in accordance to His purpose and those that bring honor and glorify Him, revealing His perfect will. Sometimes he answers. Other times he may not, or he would impress on our heart to wait. At times it may be difficult to wait, but it is for us to continue in prayer, having trust and faith, as God might want to work out certain issues in our lives before he answers our prayer.

God answers prayers according to His time and will, he follows His will for our life. His timing is not the same as ours. He knows when is the best time to answer our prayers. Waiting can be a form of testing to develop strong faith. Our dependency on Him produces patience, perseverance, and a closer relationship with Him, believing that God's timing is the best and he is in control as we continue to pray, looking to Him as our source.

Many things can hinder God from not answering our prayers. The scriptures tells us that "sin separates us from God." Sins such as, worshiping other gods, those who participate in such sin are proud in heart and self-righteous. They have iniquity in their hearts and reject the truth of God. Another is when mankind has unconfessed sins in their lives, a barrier between us and God, hindering our fellowship with Him. The scriptures warns us, "our iniquities have separation between you and God and our sins have hid His face from us, that he will not hear," wickedness places a barrier between us and God. Therefore we cannot experience His blessing in our lives (Is. 59:2).

Mankind live after the flesh, has selfish motives, and does not pray in accordance to God's will, their prayers are filled with unforgiveness and doubt. Thereby not having confidence in the power of prayer. This makes it impossible for them to have access to God. He would not hear their cries, as God hears the prayers of the righteous. Those who call upon Him in spirit and in truth (Ps. 34:13–15).

Although we were all born into sin, God does hear the prayers of sinners, especially those who genuinely call upon Him in genuine repentance, asking for His forgiveness and seeking salvation. In this instance, he would hear and answer those prayers, redeeming and placing them into His family. On occasions, God will answer to sinners' prayers when their cries are of earthly needs. And because of His mercy and grace, he would answer them out of the generosity of His compassionate heart according to the person's faith in what he or she seeks. It is important for us to know that God responds to prayers of the heart, and he encourages all mankind to seek Him with their heart, "You will seek me and find me when you seek with all your heart." God sometimes hear the prayers of sinners, for he alone reserves the right to hear whomever he desires, which only depends on their circumstances, he looks on their hearts and their cries before he answers the prayers of sinners (Jer. 29:13).

The Bible tells us that God delights to answer all of our prayers and gives us what we asked of Him when we can come to Him in submission, humility, and confidence in our prayers. His Word tells us, "If we have confidence in Him, if we ask anything according to His will, he will hear us."

It's important that, when we pray to God, we must first make sure that our lives are characterized in the standing of God, holy and acceptable unto Him, fully repentant, and genuinely serving Him, for the scriptures says, "The righteous cry, and the Lord hearth them and delivers them."

Second, make sure that our prayers are spiritually filled and lined up with God's will and not according to what we want, for the prayers of a righteous man is powerful because the eyes of the Lord are over the righteous and His ears are open unto their prayers.

Third, we ought to pray with persistence, never giving up even when we don't hear from God, rather we continually pray in faith and thanksgiving, asking in the authority of Jesus Christ who intercedes on our behalf to God the Father (1 John 5:14; Ps. 34:15,17).

Jesus exhibited to us two ways in which we can go to God in prayer. We can either go to Him publicly or secretly. Jesus while on earth did both, but for different reasons and at different times. For instance, Jesus prayed publicly after His baptism, and while praying, all who were present witnessed and heard the voice of God proclaiming Jesus as His beloved Son, seeing the heavens open and the Holy Spirit ascending on Him, confirming Jesus' true identity, the revelation of Holy Trinity, and the beginning of His earthly ministry. He publicly prayed to honor, glorify, and give thanks to God before he performed miracles, ate, or healed so the people could see His dependence and know that he and His Father were one and that he could not do anything of His own self for he sought the will of His Father. Jesus also prayed in secret many times in the Bible, such as in the garden of Gethsemane.

When Jesus prayed in secret, it was His alone time to meet God the Father to rejuvenate and strengthen His spirit, because he was in the form of a man (the flesh). Therefore he continually needed spiritual nourishment from His heavenly Father (Matt. 3:13–17, 6:6).

Jesus commanded us to pray in secret where we could have alone time with Him for it's important in our daily walk, but most importantly, it also develops the spiritual characteristics of Christ in our lives. As Christians pray publicly, we know that in our prayers, our attitude and motives must always bring attention and glorification to God and not our self and not be seen as the Pharisees that Jesus condemned in the temple. Jesus knew we are flesh and we cannot make it in this sinful world without constant communication with God in prayer. He leaves with us the blueprint on how we must pray and have an effective prayer life. As he taught His twelve disciples how they ought to pray daily (Luke 18:9–14, 11).

Our father which art in heaven

We begin by acknowledging God as our heavenly Father who is in heaven, who became our Father through our salvation, which is the new birth.

Hallowed by thy name

We acknowledge that God is holy, separate, different, and distinct from all others. This reminds us of our reverence in worship and praise toward Him.

Thy kingdom come

We pray for Jesus to come, putting an end to this evil world, and set up His kingdom on earth.

Thy will be done be done on earth as it is in heaven

We accept God's will on earth, revealing His secret plan for this universe by the revelation of His Word through the desires he places in the heart as we build up the Kingdom of God.

Give us this day our daily bread

We ask for the provisions of His people, both physical and spiritual, as we depend on Him daily for our every needs.

Forgive our sins as we forgive others

We ask for God's forgiveness so we can extend forgiveness to others.

Lead us not into temptation

We ask God for help to fight temptations so we sin not against Him.

Deliver us from Evil

We pray for God's protection and deliverance from the evils of this world and the tactics of Satan.

For thine is the Kingdom, the power and the Glory forever

We acknowledge God's greatness in this universe, knowing that all power and glory belong to Him alone, who is able to answer all our prayers.

Prayer is the best way to communicate with God, an act of worship as we express our gratitude for His loving kindness and goodness. The scriptures says the prayer of the righteous draws us closer to God, giving us power for everyday life and ministry, building us up spiritually as we recognize His provision in our lives and providing us deliverance from trouble. We must ensure that our prayers are righteous, authentic coming from a pure heart in our glorification and acknowledgment of God and proclaiming His truth, for prayer is our spiritual armor that covers us as we do battle for God.

Prayer is powerful. It is our life source, a spring life that fills us with joy and delight as we commune with God, relying on His willingness to answer and to accomplish His will through us. In our prayer, we harmonize with God's nature and character, and glorifying Him in the true spirit receiving His power, which is seen in the miraculous works he performs in our lives through our prayers.

Renewing our trust in God faithfulness, knowing that he cares and he will answer our prayers. When praying, don't be anxious for anything, but in everything in prayer and supplication with thanksgiving, let our request be made known to God, he will strengthen us to do all he desires of us and work all things out for our good and His glory (Phil. 4:6).

Prayer to God is a privilege that should inspire gratitude, reverence, and humility

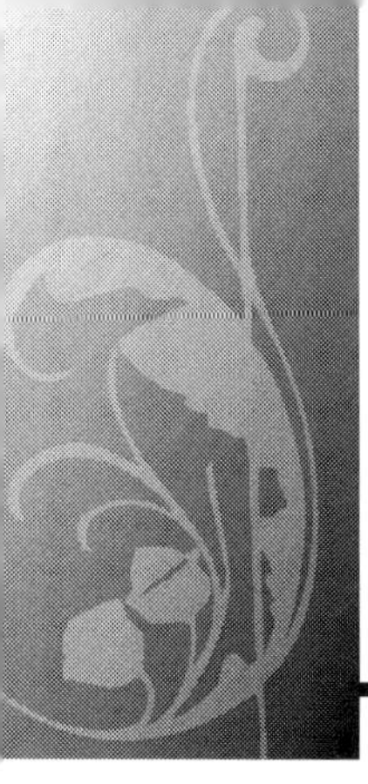

Walking with God

Walking with God is when a person is in oneness with Him and pleasing Him. He is absolutely dependent, devoted, and in obedience to God. Becoming fellow laborers with Christ. Demonstrating and have deep faith in the gospel of Christ through daily communion and fellowship with God through prayer, meditation, and, most importantly, His Word patterning our whole entire life after Jesus Christ. Trusting Him completely. Being humble, faithful, and loyal to God while walking in the Spirit, His ways, and becoming mature in our Christian walk. Dedicated to fulfilling His will, seeking to live a blameless life and keeping our mind on Christ. God told Abraham, "Walk perfect before Him." Therefore in walking with God, the Word of God must be cemented in our hearts and minds, establishing in us a strong partnership with God. (Gen. 17:1).

Having an intense spiritual pursuit of God and developing a servant's heart to follow hard after Christ. We commune with Him in every facet of our lives, letting go of anything that may distract us from God. Standing in agreement with Him and His Word as we walk with Him, the scriptures asks, "Can two walk together, except they be agreed?" for God desires for us to walk humbly before Him, acting justly and loving with mercy.

Displaying genuine love, compassion, treat others fairly, dressed in humility, revering God, focusing on Him as sovereignty, pleasing Him in everything. Having a vast knowledge of God, motivated in sharing His Word, while in the process enriching the hearts of mankind and leading them to the light, which can only be found in Jesus Christ. Our everyday life should always be patterned after Christ, following in His footsteps, emulating the things he did while on earth, resisting sin, keeping His commandments, obeying His voice, and serving and cleaving unto Him (Amos 3:3).

In our walk with God, it's all about pleasing Him and promoting the glory of Christ through the life we live, with our entire lives under the direction of God, setting our minds on the spirit of Christ. Adopting His viewpoints, which will lead us towards His will and plans. As we continue to walk with Him, he will slowly unfold the secrets of heaven through the Spirit, by giving us His wisdom and revealing to us His glory as we explore the riches of knowing Him on a deeper level. Discovering the true delights of walking with God. Separating ourselves from the things of this world, portraying and displaying Christ in and through our lives by our actions, attitudes, and the Christ-like attributes that place Christ in a positive way, remaining focused to what he has called us to do. Thereby living godly and righteous lives, continuing to trust and glorifying God in all things, laying aside anything that might weigh us down, hinder, or trap us, as we look unto Jesus, for we know our future is in heaven and not in this world (Heb. 12:1).

Walking with God is a lifelong test of faith. Therefore, we practice patience and demonstrate perseverance and endurance, placing our attentions, thoughts, energy, and values on the things of God while we live spiritually in the presence of God as he accomplishes His will through us. It is having an intimate relationship with God through faith in His Son Jesus Christ, yearning to know Him, sharing our life with Him, and hearing His voice, all of these are absolutely necessary for us to walk perfect before Christ. Always in close proximity with Christ, regarding Him as our everything, aligning our will with His and exercising our faith in Him accompanied with our obedience. Fearing God in our hearts, believing in His goodness, drawing closer to Him through earnest prayer and a genuine love for Him. Consequently, God then will preserves us from bad influences as His presence is always with us. He becomes to us the comforting, supporting and sympathizing friend as he protects our lives, giving us the peaceful assurance of His everlasting love (1 John 2:6).

Walking in the likeness of Jesus Christ, for we are the embodiment of Him, exhibiting the characteristics of Him in humility and righteousness. Speaking the truth, always presenting our lives as a sacrifice holy unto God in our need to serve and our willingness to forgive others, thereby establishing inner spiritual growth maturing in biblical knowledge and contributing to the development of the body of Christ.

In walking with God, we're always ready at any given time to defend God and His Word and bring glory to Him. Therefore in whatever we do, eat, or drink, we must do it all to the glory of God, for His ways are reflected in our thoughts, actions, motivation, and life choices as a result of our genuine relationship with Him. In the process of walking with God, we are challenged to change the minds of those living in sin. By exposing sin and speaking the truth about their sins with compelling and strong facts, which are based on God's Word, while displaying an expression of a calm exterior in Christ Jesus. Exhibiting patience and godliness and maintaining self-control as we walk with God (Matt. 5:16).

As we walk pleasing unto God, our desires are to produce the fruits of the spirit so that the world will recognize us as true followers of Christ, which in turn serves as a positive influence to others by us choosing to live according to the standards of God. Being conformed to God standards in moral characters, living righteously according to His holy law, and walking in faith. Focusing on the greatness of God as the Holy Spirit motivates, guides, giving us the courage and strength needed to walk. Listening to His directives, having clear discernment of Him and confidence in the truth of His Word. Receiving His boldness in the teaching of His Word and making a difference to a person's life. As we walk with God, the light of His glory is revealed in us, allowing the Spirit to direct our minds and maintain our walk. We have persistence in spite of the different obstacles, trials, and temptations that may come our way. Fighting and persevering for God as we walk, delighting in our past blessings. Becoming ever so more determined to our devotion to God, allowing nothing to stop us from accomplishing what God purpose for us in our walk with Him (2 Cor. 5:17).

Walking with God is not always going to be easy. There will be rough patches along the way. Jesus tells us, "If we are not of the world, the world would hate us." Therefore we must keep on encouraging ourselves by reading and memorizing on the stories of the Old Testament Saints who have walked with God faithfully, never gave up but steadfastly continued to trust in God with strong faith despite all their circumstances. Those stories are testimonies which makes us more determined in our commitment and dedication to God. As the old-time saints were victorious, we too shall be, because the same God that was with them in their walk is with us today, he changed not and he will never leave us, if we remain faithful to Him. We are built on the firm and solid foundation that can only be found in Christ Jesus. We see through His eyes and not the eyes of man. We walk in the standard of the fruits of the spirit, identifying ourselves with Christ in our conducts, behavior, choices, having the assurance that our life is pleasing to Him. Loving the things he loves and hating the things he hates, remaining loyal and standing firm in our faith, the scripture admonish us "to be steadfast, unmovable, always abounding in the work of the Lord, for our labor is not vain in the Lord" (1 Cor. 15:58; Gen. 6–7).

By walking with God, we are automatically at odds with the world, because we are followers of Christ, separated from this world. Therefore we engulf ourselves with matters that pertains to God and cleave to the teachings of His Word for direction. We are seen now as an enemy to the world and would be subjected to mockery, betrayal, and loneliness as we stand up for biblical truths and God. However, though we be rejected or cast aside for Christ's sake, we can still rejoice in our hearts for those suffering received on earth, because great will be our rewards in heaven when we spend eternity in the presence of God.

It's vital while walking with God and having the willingness to follow Him, that we hold on to His every move, calling on the Holy Spirit to show us the way as we make decisions in life and responding to everything the way Jesus would. The world out there is watching our every move and ready to devour us at any given time. Therefore in our daily walk with God, it's not about ourselves. Instead, it's all about God. What we produce and how we care and communicate to others should all co-exist with Him,thus bringing glory to God. Walking circumspectly not as fools but wise walking in the truth of God (Eph. 5:15).

The Bible illustrates two such persons who walked with God and are mentioned in the Hall of Faith: Enoch and Noah. The scriptures say that Enoch walked with God for he was a preacher of righteousness standing firm against unrighteousness and immorality by warning the people of his generation of God's judgment. Enoch pleased God for he had a close relationship with Him. He walked by faith, trusting and embracing God's ways, for he excelled in godliness. And for his faithfulness, God took him out of this world, and he never experienced death. Noah, the great-grandson of Enoch, was a righteous man who feared and communed with God, like his great-grandfather Enoch. He too also lived in a time where his generation was wicked and evil (Gen. 5:24; Jude 14–15).

Noah lived in the time period where corruption and wickedness filled the world, for the scriptures tell us, "God saw that every imagination of the thoughts of man heart was only evil continually." God wanted to destroy mankind, but Noah found grace in the eyes of the Lord according to the Word of God. He was a just man, perfect in his generation, and he walked with God. Noah separated himself from the sins of his perverse generation that was all around him, for he feared God. He continued to live a righteous life through faith in God. God's grace characterized Noah's life. He had a love for righteousness and a hatred for wickedness as he walked faithfully and had an intimate relationship with God. He was obedient to God's Word. Hence, when God told him to build an Ark for he was going to destroy the world, Noah, because of his great faith and trust in God, even at 500 years old he began building the Ark. While building the Ark, he started to preach repentance, warning the people of the coming wrath of God, yet they chose not to heed his word but continued in their wickedness instead of repenting (1 Peter 2:5).

The people mocked and made fun of him as he continued to build the Ark and preach of the righteousness of God, repentance, and the coming flood. Noah never allowed the people to hinder his obedience and faith in the covenant that God made with him. Rather he continued to keep his integrity and faith, being blameless and devoted towards God as he listened, trusted, and believed in what God commanded of him. Thereby when God began to pour out his wrath on the earth with the flood, he extended his saving grace towards Noah and his family, thus preserving human life on earth.

Noah lived an exemplary life. He demonstrated the vital importance of being obedient and faithful to God without asking questions, he continued trusting in God and doing all he had commanded. (Gen. 6:22).

The scripture tells us, after the flood, Noah built an Altar unto God and offered sacrifices to Him, which demonstrated his humbleness, devotion, and faithfulness, and showed his act of worship and gratitude to

God for the preserving of his family. Noah's faith, trust, and obedience are valuable lessons on how to walk righteously before God, no matter the age and circumstance we face. When we remain faithful with our whole heart, desiring to follow Christ, he will then place His grace and favor all over our lives to sustain us. Noah had an intimate and vibrant relationship with God. His life is an example for faith and righteous living, and God's protection provides a refuge for those who faithfully serve Him. Also Noah having a reverent, faithful, and worshipful relationship with God shows the truth of the gospel that it is grace that saves us through faith, for the grace of God was upon his life as his entire family was saved and protected from the flood (Gen. 8:20).

As we continue to walk with God, we become Ambassadors for Him, thereby offering to this sinful world the choice of reconciliation with Christ by the repenting of sins and embracing God's way in every aspect of life. We teach and preach righteousness, denounce sin and the sinful lifestyle of this world, warning them of the coming judgment of Christ, so like Noah and his family, they too can be rescued for the wrath of God. Therefore as we walk with God, it becomes our duty to live and uphold biblical standards, and not be accommodating to the trends and value of this world but continue to walk in humility before God. Walking in the power of the Holy Spirit of Christ as he continues to guide, strengthen, protect, and make our paths straight so we can be successful in this walk, for it's not how we start our walk with God but how we finish it. (2 Cor. 5:20).

Obedience, faithfulness, circumcision of the heart, and newness of mind are the ingredients for successfully walking with God.

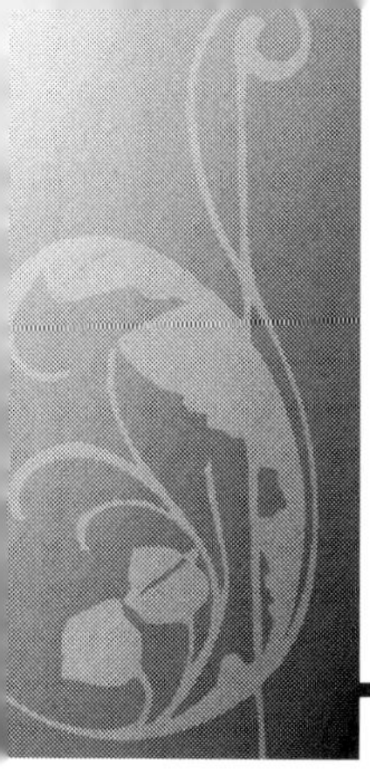

Living by Faith

The Word of God tells us, "Faith is the substance of things hoped for, the evidence of things not seen." Faith is trusting God in all circumstances, believing that he would be faithful to His promises. Faith is an outward action that reveals our inward attitude, which is evident in our obedience to God. By faith we gain knowledge, that the Word of God framed the earth. Faith is important for salvation, it's only by God's grace through faith can mankind be saved, believing in God's grace through the shed blood of Jesus Christ on the cross. Faith and obedience are inseparable, they cannot work without one another, it's truly believing and obeying God's Word. The scriptures tell us, "Without faith it is impossible to please God." Therefore, our faith in God is necessary, it maintains His divine presence in our lives and our constant connection to Him as we acknowledge and embrace His existence (Eph. 2:8; Heb. 11:1,6).

Saving faith is the channel through which we receive salvation, trusting completely in Jesus Christ's redemptive work on the cross, the only way that anyone can have God's grace in their lives. Our faith through Christ expresses itself in love and actively resists sin from our lives, showing concern for the work of Christ and connecting Him to us. In obtaining saving faith in Christ, we believe in the provision that God has offered to us through His son Jesus Christ. Thirsting and hungering for more of Him, wanting to know Him in an intimate way, thereby having a strong desire to serve Him with our whole heart. Putting aside the present comfort of life for a future reward in heaven as we become God minded, looking toward eternity. Our faith in God is not limited to what we can see, for the object of our faith is Jesus Christ. With

Him, nothing is impossible. We make choices in faith that ensure greater reward throughout eternity (Luke 17:6).

True faith includes personal dedication to Christ, it requires risk and uncertainty, intensely trusting and obeying God. Pursuing after Him and His righteousness, reverently worshiping Him in all honesty, believing God and His Word, in all situation, even when we can't see the outcome, rather we remain confident in God and His promises. Determined to be strong and devoted to Him. This faith unites believers with Christ, purifying the heart as we work in godliness with holy affections and patience. Thereby growing stronger in the knowledge of His ways and our faith (2 Cor. 5:7).

Establishing a right relationship with God is essential to living a life of faith, for a righteous person is justified by his or her faith in God, the scriptures say, "The just shall live by faith." Relying firmly on God's law, His righteous principles, and promises, building strong faith, placing our hope in Him, as he equips us to accept His calling on our lives not knowing where it will lead us, yet we keep our eyes on Him.

Living by faith is spiritual. It's having confidence in God; believing he will perform that which pertains to His will; growing, maturing, and progressing in righteousness; exhibiting confidence in the righteous characteristics that fosters hope and truth. Maintaining His grace of sanctification in us where we can look beyond our present situation to a fervent hope in God with the comforting of His Holy Spirit, elevating us from one level of maturity to another (Rom. 1:17).

Faith in God helps us to overcome difficulties, bestowing within us the power source needed in this world, the stepping-stone of courage, as we base our lives upon faith. Persevering our lives by faith through His Word, exercising patience, living a spiritual -filled life, developing our inward and outward faith as we walk in the fullness of God's grace. As he makes our pathway prosperous, filled with everlasting joy. God sees the hearts of every believer, and the extent of our faith leads us to be accepted by God as His children and also as righteous men before Him, the scripture tells us Abraham believed God, and it was counted unto him for righteousness (Rom. 4:3).

Therefore, we continue to formulate our lives only on faith in Jesus Christ and His righteousness and not in the theories of mankind, for we begin our walk with Christ on faith. Mankind must live out faith based on their inward righteousness through the indwelling of the Holy Spirit. Our righteousness comes from God. Our faith reveals God in us as we continue life in Him, never returning to this evil world. Continuing to hope in the glory that is yet to come and our future home in heaven. Having a clearer understanding of eternal realities, experiencing God's power as we act on faith in making decisions and choices deriving them from His Word. Focusing not on the things that are visible. Instead we focus on Jesus Christ. As we live in faith, the Holy Spirit of Christ helps, encourages, preserves us in testing, strengthens, and allows us to make choices that ensure a greater reward as we live righteously in faith, even unto the very end (Heb. 10:38).

Faith in God produces results. It is the work of God in the hearts of His followers as we display deep confidence and commitment to Him and His Word. Dependent on Him in everything, for scriptures tell us, "Apart from God we cannot do nothing." With faith, we realize we can do great work for God, having full understanding of the power of faith, thereby enabling us to do miraculous work for Him. Faith only comes alive when we act on what we believe accompanying with absolute trust in God.

Faith without work is dead. Lack of work reveals an unchanged heart, a life without the Holy Spirit of God. In possessing faith in our lives it will always results in a transformed life, which is demonstrated in our good works,obedience to God which is the mark of having genuine faith (1 John 5:4; James 2:26).

In balancing faith with work, we see ourselves clearly through God's Word, figuring out who we are in Him thus making positive changes to our lives. Faith always activates action. Anyone can have faith; however, it's what they do to make faith come to life. God gives us faith based on His love, wisdom, and grace. Therefore, whatever we do in faith must always bring honor and glory to Him, letting our light to shine in the world even when they are against us.

Standing firm in our faith, unmovable and unshakable, even when it seems like all is lost, for we know Jesus Christ is the source of our faith, and we do nothing without Him. In trying times, our faith flourishes. The more we become the spiritual heirs of Abraham, holding fast to God's Word by faith. We live a full spiritual life each day, allowing our faith to be evident and observable to others as it grows in our heart and manifests in our works (Gal. 3:29).

Believers living by faith, the scriptures tell us, "We are protected by the power of God." The armor of God is our protective barrier to recognize Satan's deceptiveness and tactics, destroying them before they destroy our relationship with God. The armor of God has different parts: the belt of truth, breastplate of righteousness, shoe of the gospel of peace, shield of faith, helmet of salvation, and the sword of the Spirit. This armor is essential to withstand the darts that the evil one throws at us. Hence, they are necessary, not only to protect but also help us to stand firm in our faith as we remain faithful to God. As followers of Christ, we encounter spiritual warfare of our faith with Satan, he opposes the things of God and seeks the downfall of the people of God. Hence, the importance for us to be equip to stand against Satan and to live a spirit-empowered life (Eph. 6:10–12).

The breastplate of righteousness requires genuine holiness in our heart and mind, being in a right standing with God, wrapped up in His righteousness. Safeguarding our minds leaving no space, so that Satan can't corrupt it with doubt and the impurities of this world. To Live in faith, we must be in all readiness to stand up for the truth of the gospel of God, having full knowledge and understanding of the Word, being renewed in our mind. Exhorting the truth with confidence, in our sanctification and speaking the truth in all readiness. The shoe of peace is confident that we are at peace with God and being reconciled to Him through faith. Standing firm in His power, having our feet on the solid rock which is Jesus Christ.

The shield of faith protects our spiritual lives. Our complete trust and faith in God's Word extinguishes the arrows of the enemy. We place our hope in our salvation being justified and free from sin, knowing one day we will spend eternity with Him, for we're under His grace. The sword of the Spirit, is the holiness and power of God's Word, it cuts deep into the souls and judges the heart of mankind, thereby transforming them into a new creations of God (John 8:44; Heb. 4:12).

Living life by faith, we are dressed in the complete divine protection and armor of God. Putting on His image in all truth, righteousness, peace, and faith, energized by His Word, growing spiritually in strength and Christian virtues. We are able to control our mind in prayer, by remaining faithful in the true gospel and grace. Building up our strength in the Lord, enduring and hope in God, for we are more than conquerors through him that loved us. Looking at life as a battleground, always be alert to defend our faith, praying earnestly so we can detect, discern, and deflect the enemy and be spiritually victorious (Eph. 4:15).

The Bible tells us that Abraham had genuine faith in God. He trusted in the promises of God and acted accordingly in obedience and faith. God called Abraham to leave his country, family, his father's house, and made a promise unto him. Abraham believed and trusted the Word of God, his care, and guidance, and so by faith, he obeyed God and departed to a land unknown to him.

Abraham demonstrated his faith in his action by listening to God, which led him to adhere to His divine will, submitting his heart and mind to God's Word as he faithfully obeyed God. Abraham believed that God would be faithful to His promises and knew that his faith was in the one who had proven himself to be true. Even at the age of one hundred, he believed God's promise of a son with his wife Sarah, which was fulfilled by God (Gen. 12).

Abraham's greatest revelation of his genuine faith came when God told him to offer up his son, Isaac, as a sacrifice unto him. Despite his deep love for his son Isaac, Abraham had a greater love for God. Thus he did not rebel or resist God's command, but instead he continued to be faithful to God, for he believed that God would raise his son back to life.

Abraham was committed to God. He had a personal relationship with God. Even in adversities and testing, he demonstrated genuine obedience, trust, and faithfulness to God. Thus, the scriptures say, "He was a friend of God." Abraham exhibited an extraordinary level of genuine faith in God. Abraham's life stands as a biblical illustration of truth that our salvation is based on God's grace through faith, he believed and trusted in God's promises and God reckoned him as a righteous man. Abraham earned justification by his faith in God, which propelled him to move. He did not have to work for faith because it was proven by his actions, as his heart was fixed on eternity, and his faith allowed him to look beyond this present world to a future home in heaven (Heb. 11:10).

Living by faith is important as it is pleasing to God, we demonstrate to Him our dependence, belief, while in the process exhibiting our faithfulness and trust in Him, as we recognize our inabilities and weaknesses. Listening, believing, and obeying Him, stepping out on faith that can move mountain, knowing nothing is impossible with God. Faith is a work of God, it creates a divine awareness in our hearts, putting us under the control of God, so we can accomplish His will and express His love, therefore our faith can not be used for selfish interest or earthly gains. Our faith is the essence of a spiritual life and the entrance to forming a strong lasting relationship with God, it's our devotion and attachment to Christ, expressed in our love, trust and gratitude.

True faith is expressed in our obedience to God, resulting in our works of righteousness.

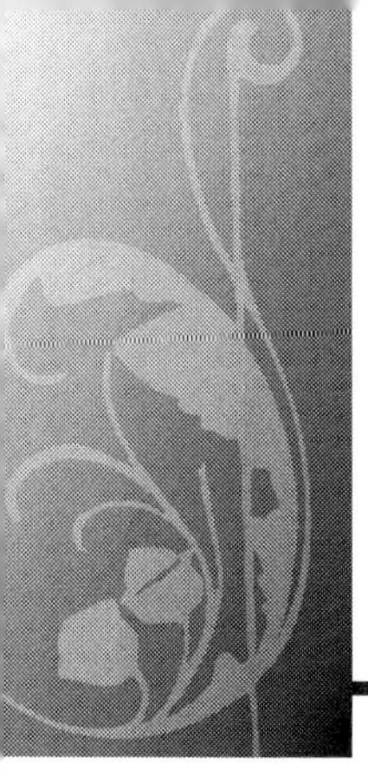

Roadblocks in Our Paths

Roadblocks are obstacles that hinder a Christian spiritual maturity in Christ and keeps them from achieving the plans that God has set out for their lives. If not looked at carefully, it has the potential of destroying lives throughout eternity. Roadblocks come into our lives in different sizes and ways, they can either be naturally or spiritually. Therefore, it's imperative that we discern them for they reminds us of our own weakness and our need for dependence on God, The Bible says, "the mind of a man plans his ways, but the Lord shows him what to do." We must rest assured that our present and future are in God's hand as he lightens our pathway. At times, God will allow spiritual roadblocks to come into our lives for various reasons, to protect us or to build up our character, correction, direction, sin, and dependence on Him (Prov. 6:7).

In other instances, roadblocks enter our lives due to our disobedience to God or lack of knowledge of His Word, for purification thereby testing our faith in Him, for building up compassion toward others and to be more thankful. But most of all, roadblocks are to humble and remind us that God is still in control. It's only through our trying times can we learn to appreciate who we are in Christ Jesus, our willingness to abide by His rule and recognizing His faithfulness in our prayers. Roadblocks comes into our lives for a specific purpose, as we have been approved by God and is lacking nothing in Christ Jesus, for "all thing work together for good to them that love God and are called unto His purpose." We must recognize that our roadblocks are a part of God's divine purpose and is inevitable for Christians, therefore we must ensure that we are continually growing spiritually in the likeness of His Son Jesus Christ.

Roadblocks does not show how faithful we are to God, but instead, how faithful we will remain to God. Roadblocks work together only for our good if we remain steadfast in Christ, His righteousness. We must be alert, wise in heart and in the knowledge of Christ, to face our roadblocks head-on with positive affirmation, confident and encouraged by the Word, not looking at the size of our roadblock. Knowing that God is bigger than our roadblocks, and His faithfulness, will make a way of escape. Therefore, when encountering roadblocks, speak positive affirmations, always remembering that life and death is in the power of the tongue. Be encouraged in the Word, put our focus on God and not our circumstances, trusting in His wisdom to deal with our roadblocks, depending solely on His power and guidance. Realigning our hearts and minds with God's Word, leaving no room for wrongdoing or evil thoughts. Fully aware that roadblocks delay the plans of God in our lives, therefore we must walk away from the power of sin, releasing anything that will prohibit us from following after God's (1 Cor. 10:13).

God places roadblocks in our life for His purpose and he chose us. In this process, he works through us so that our testimonies can be an encouragement to others, thereby bringing glory to Him. At some point our roadblocks could be painful, as God allows us to share in His sufferings, in the process it form the kind of character he desires as he blesses, preserves and redirects our lives assuring us of His ever-present love. We now view our roadblocks in a different perspective, fighting them in the power of Christ, using the spiritual approach through fervent prayer and fasting along with the leading of the Holy Spirit. Depending on God for he will never forsake us, instead he'll be our helper encouraging us to remain strong, courageous, and to continue persevering through our roadblocks, as he walks us through the valley and bringing us safely out on the other side (Deut. 31:8).

We must not be ignorant to the fact that not all roadblocks are from God. Therefore, it is essential that we discern which roadblock is of God and which is of Satan, for there are differences to them, one leads to destruction and the other brings transformation of life and growth. As roadblocks enters into our lives, it's very important for us not to be angry with God. Firstly, we must identify the source of the roadblock through prayer and supplication, because in our own humanistic abilities we are limited in strength and rendered powerless, thus the need to acquire God's divine intervention on our next move in facing the roadblock.

There are different causes for roadblocks. It could be as a result of sin or pride, which can be either temporary or permanent. It's according to how mankind deals with them, roadblocks occur because of mankind's unwillingness to be truly delivered as they believe their beyond help. To conquer roadblocks, it all depends on our choice either we want to be free from them with the help of the Holy Spirit or continue to fight in our own spirit and stay in them. The choices made will either lead to newness of life in Christ or self-destruction,and eternal damnation due to pride and lack of spiritual discernment (Is. 59:2).

Roadblocks that enter into person's life could prevent him or her from going to hell. However, it is all based on their choice, whether or not they ignore those signs given, the scripture tells us, "God is long suffering towards us not willing that any should perish." Thus he places roadblocks as a deterrent. God also puts roadblocks in our lives to keep us safe, as our lives are reckless and careless before Him, and also because he loves and cares for us. He knows what's best for us. Roadblocks from God are given to mankind as another chance of obtaining eternal life with Christ; however, despite God's efforts, mankind refuses to take heed of such an opportunity which places Christ in their lives. Not realizing that the roadblock placed in their lives were for their own good, protection, and benefit, rather they choose to be frustrated, angry at God and refuse come to terms with their sins, allowing it to take over their lives.

There are many stories in the Bible of persons who experienced roadblocks in their lives, such as Saul, who is better known as the apostle Paul. Before God changed his name to Paul, Saul was a man who was persecuting and killing the people of God. One night on the road to Damascus to persecute more Christians, Jesus Christ met Saul and asked him, "Why you persecute me?" Saul recognized that it was the voice of God, he repented and adhered to the commands of Christ, dedicating his life from that moment to obeying Christ. As a result of his obedience to God, Paul is known throughout to all Christians and the New Testament as the greatest apostle of Christ. Paul recognized his roadblock was from God. He responded to Jesus' call to be a minster, a witness for him and the gospel of Christ, thus he went out preaching and teaching the Word of God, having no regard for his own life, remaining committed to Christ (Acts 9, 26:14).

The Bible also tells another story of a man named of Balaam and the talking donkey. God placed a roadblock in his path, thus saving him from destruction. Balaam was a prophet who heard from God; however, because his heart was not right with God, he led the people of Israel astray, he was known as a wicked and false prophet. King Balak wanted to place a curse on the people of Israel, so he sent for Balaam. God came to Balaam and told him not to go. Despite God's warning, Balaam decided to go, because he would be rewarded with a house filled with silver and gold. Balaam allowed greed and wealth to make him disobey God. On his way to meet with King Balak who was at war with the people of Israel, God placed a roadblock in his path. The donkey saw the roadblock and stop for he could not continue on the journey, Balaam was filled with anger and rage, he began to beat the donkey, instead of realizing that God was trying to stop him.

Not only did God place that roadblock into his path, he also demonstrated his miraculous power by making the donkey speak to Balaam. Yet, Balaam was still blinded to his sinful nature, and did not recognize God in his present situation. It's Only when God opened his eyes, he saw the angel of God standing in the path with his sword drawn. Had it not been for the donkey, the angel of God was going to kill Balaam. Balaam then humble himself, acknowledge his sins, repented and did as the angel of the Lord had commanded.

God allowed Balaam to continue on his journey to meet with King Balak; however, Balaam did not curse the people of Israel, instead he asked king Balak, "Shall I curse, whom God hath not curse?" He told the king he that could only speak what God put in his mouth to say.

The spirit of the Lord came upon Balaam. He spoke the message that he received from God, and poured out blessings on Israel. He also continued prophesying blessing upon the people of Israel and foretold the coming of the Messiah, thereby bringing glory and honor unto God (Numbers 23–24).

This strongly demonstrates that God is more than willing to bring us down to our knees if we continue to ignore the roadblocks that he places in our lives. Therefore, being stubborn to God's roadblocks will only result in pain, hurt, grief and heartache, thus the need to evaluate roadblocks to see if God is trying to get our attention. If we realize that the roadblocks we're facing in our lives are of God, we must then humble ourselves, repent of our sins and submit our lives to Christ. He will order our steps, giving us the strength, and courage needed to be successful in whatever he purposed for us.

Roadblocks can be destructive or a blessing; discern your roadblocks to be able to fight effectively.

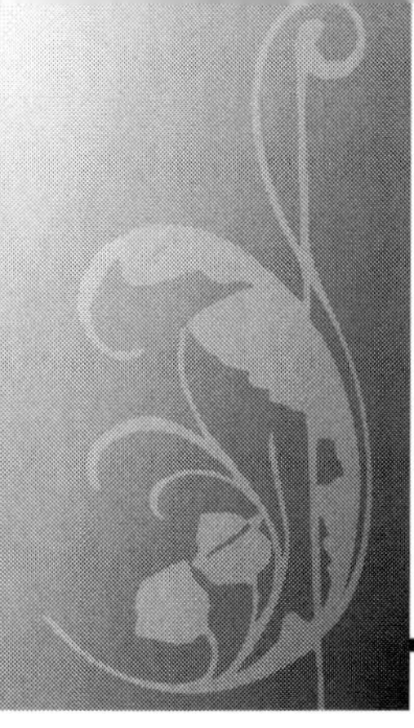

Fear Factor

Fear is a paralyzing, crippling feeling that can destroy a person's life, it is a destructive force. Fear in of itself is a sin; thus, fear is listed in the book of Revelation as one of the sins that can send a person to hell. Persons will be cast into the lake of fire because of fear, for it violates the first commandment of God, which is to love thy God. Fear is a thought or an imagination that is activated into something that can either be positive or negative depending on how it is viewed in our lives. The Bible tells us about two type of fear: the fear of God and the fear of the Spirit, they are completely different. The fear of God is beneficial to living a life with God, whereby we revere His power, glory and respect His wrath and anger towards sin. The fear of the spirit is harmful, dangerous, and destructive that needs to be addressed immediately, it is one of Satan's most popular weapon that he uses on mankind and especially against the believers in Christ. Hence, why God repeatedly tells us through His Word to "fear not" and "he have not given us a spirit of fear but of power, love and of a sound mind" (2 Tim. 1:7; Rev. 21:8).

The fear of God does not mean for us to be afraid or terrified of Him. Instead we ought to trust, respect, and be in awe of Him. Acknowledging all His attributes and what he truly represents, which then leads to a life of peace, contentment, and safety. Fearing God for both Christians and non-Christians is to have full understanding of God's hatred towards sin and His judgment of sin. God is not a respecter of person when it comes to the judging sin.

The fear God is the beginning of wisdom. We cannot fear Him unless we totally understand who he is and what he stands for, it's only through that process can we understand the consequences of disobedience to Him. We now have an inner awareness of the sanctity of life, leading to wisdom, which ultimately reveals itself in the love of God through His Son Jesus Christ. We begin doing good works protruding from the heart with genuine desire to honor God, with reverential trust, knowledge and understanding of His greatness and showing respect to His mighty power. Therefore, in fearing God, we need not be afraid (Prov. 19:13).

Fearing God plays a positive influence in the life of Christians, it allows us to live in total holiness, thus hindering us from giving into our sinful nature. To fear God is to love Him, cling and learn from Him. Fearing God is us being directed in our response to His Word, it's an inducement of obedience and service to Him with the proper recognition of His sovereignty. The Bible tells us that the fear of the God is a fountain of life. It is strong, confident, and a place of refuge for us to depart from sin and seek forgiveness so we don't encounter His wrath but rather receive His gift of salvation.

Fear God is a life choice we must make as mankind, by choosing to fear Him, we receive His strength and power. He guards us from spiritual danger, provides His divine protection as His angel keeps us safe from destruction, and enabling us to overcome all the fears of life, as the Word encourages us many times to fear not (Prov. 8:13).

In fearing God, we walk in all His ways and love Him, as it is impossible to love Him and not fear Him for these two component complement each other. Placing all our hope and desires in Him, believing His promises as we await to see them fulfilled in our lives, the Scripture tells us "God is love, and there is no fear in love, for love cast out all fear". The fear of God keeps us from defiling our conscience of committing sin, causing us to be disciplined by restraining our tongue from saying words, which is contradictory to His Word (Deut. 10:12).

The fear of God brings changes and holy alignment in our life so we can embrace righteousness, truth, and the outpouring of the Spirit of God. It helps us to overcome and fulfill everything that God has planned and purposed for our life so we can boldly enter His presence in faith and serve Him in good conscience. Motivated not by fear but by God's love, our deep respect, appreciation of Him, and His Word, which enables us to fully be aware of His judgment to those who choose not to fear Him.

We surrender our all to God, serving Him, loving Him and beholding all of His glory and majesty. Elevated to genuinely commune with Him in love, for he alone holds life and death in His hand, the scriptures tells us, "Fear not them who can only kill the body but rather fear Him who can destroy both the body and the soul" (Matt. 10:28).

The second type of fear is known as the spirit of fear. It is a spiritual force which is expressed as worry, anxiety, panic, etc, these are few of the tricks that Satan uses on mankind in hopes of trying to control the followers of Christ, and hinders some from serving God. The fear of the spirit is a powerful spirit that Satan instills inside the minds of mankind to cause doubts, unbelief and lack of trust in Christ, which creates a spiritual battle between the mind and the spirit. This spiritual battle can only be remedied with spiritual weapons because we are fighting with Satan, who wants to keep mankind away from God. The spirit of fear robs Christians of their identity in Christ, thus making it difficult to recognize the powers of God in their lives, as their focus is no longer on God but rather on their problems. In the case of non-Christians, the spirit of fear totally destroys their whole life as they simply gives in to their own fears (Eph. 6:12).

Christians who are lacking in his or her faith gives Satan the avenue he needs to attack them, because they took their eyes off God, so they become vulnerable prey for Satan. The scriptures tell, "For God's people are destroyed for lack of knowledge." Not having enough faith in the Word of God, and giving Satan room to deceive them with his half-truths and lies. It vital to know that lack of faith fosters doubt, and doubt produces unbelief as Satan twists the truth, causing Christians to question the validity of God's Word and His existence. We must be cognizant of the fact that both faith and fear come from hearing. They are manifested from what we hear, which then becomes a thought in our minds then enters into our hearts, hence, it automatically becomes a matter of choice of which one we believe to be—the truth of God's Word or the lies of Satan (Hos. 4:6; Rom. 10:17).

It is incumbent that we be careful of what we listen to and put in our minds. We ensure our minds and thoughts are filled with the word of truth and the things of God, so that the Devil cannot infiltrate them. Our faith in God upholds, nourishes, and sustains our inner man, replacing any fears that may be lurking around with positive assertion of God's

Word, consequently bringing all our thoughts into alignment with God. Rejecting evil and deceptive thoughts by saying no to Satan, praying and asking God to take those thoughts away from us, and start thinking positive thoughts that can uplift and enlighten our minds. Realizing the amount of power that we hold, as Christians operate not in the flesh but in the spirit of God, equipped with power to overcome the spirit of fear and Satan (2 Cor. 10:5).

For nonbelievers, this is one of Satan's signature tactics that he uses to keep them in his grasp and under his control. He first would begin with the mind and their imagination as he infiltrates a disastrous thought into their mind, tricking them into believing his lies that something is wrong, creating them to be fearful. That fearful thought overpowers them, taking full control of their whole life and robbing them of their joy.

Satan knows that the flesh and the minds of humans are weak. He uses them as his main tool to destroy mankind while in the process making them weak, powerless, and under his spiritual bondage. Fear of the spirit leads to fearfulness. Such fear was demonstrated in the garden of Eden when Satan caused Eve to doubt God as she ate from the tree of life, which Adam also partake of, resulting in them sinning and disobeying God. After they realized the gravity of their sin, they became fearful and hid from God. However, it was too late because they knew they had lost their spiritual connection, for their eyes were open to their nakedness (Gen. 3:10).

Satan places the spirit of fear in the minds of mankind, which causes terror, as they solely depend on worldly doctrine, walking in their own theologies and blinding their eyes to the truth of God's Word, as he continues to lead them down the road of destruction into hellfire.

As mankind allow Satan to place such fear into their minds, he will continue to feed their minds with more destructive thoughts, making them weaker and more terrified with no way of escaping. Thus the scriptures tell us, "The Devil comes to steal, kill and destroy lives." What Satan does is fulfill the desires of mankind's fleshly nature by making them feel that there is no God in heaven or they can create their own god with their imagination, thus distracting their minds.

However, there is good news for mankind under the bondage of the spirit of fear. The God of heaven has the power to help them, no one is out of His reach, and he can set them free of the spirit of fear, but only if they choose God, believe in His Son Jesus Christ, and repent of their sins. Thus scriptures tell us, "The secret of the Lord is with them that fear Him; and he will shew them His covenant" (2 Peter 3:9; John 10:10).

To overcome fear, mankind must go to the throne of grace and seek God's help in prayer, surrendering all fears over to Him, basing their prayers on His mercy, grace, power, to deliver and give them peace of mind. Confronting our fears with confidence by adjusting the way we think, be honest with ourselves about our fears, for the Scripture says " God has not given us a spirit of fear, but of power, love, and a sound mind". Our eyes and ears, are the two elements that leads the mind and soul, therefore we must guard them for they are the access to faith and fear which will eventually affect the body both physically and spiritually. Our faith and fear of God assures us of His love, the more we trust His divine sovereignty, the less fearful we become, and the devil will flee from us. Faith in Christ is the only remedy for fear, the spiritual power needed to overcome the spirit of fear (James 4:7; Job 31:1).

King David, the beloved of God, was a mighty and fearless warrior who killed the giant Goliath as a teenager. He is the man in whom we find the lineage of Jesus Christ. The Bible tells us that David struggled with fear of the spirit, despair, and depression. King David even pretended to be a madman at one point, to spare his life from King Achish. He also was afraid for his life and run from King Saul. King David also ran for his son Absolam, instead of relying and trusting in God, he gave in to the fear of spirit.

Although King David was fearful and depressed, running from his son at some point in his life, he decided not to put his trust in himself nor his army. He placed his trust in God, believing and hoping for his help. God, in turn, delivered David by using many of King David's friends, such as Hushai, to frustrate the council of Ahithophel and Joab to kill Absolam so that God could fulfill His plans for David's life (2 Sam. 12–18).

Throughout all David's fears, he remembered how God had made him victorious over all his enemies when he completely trusted, depended, and listened to him. As such he wrote many psalms, which minister to others on how to overcome fear by trusting in God. In King David's last word to the people of Israel, he spoke these words "The spirit of the Lord spake by me, and His word was in my tongue, the God of Israel said, the Rock of Israel spake to me, he that ruleth over man must be just, ruling in the fear of God."

Followers of Christ must be very careful, because the moment we take our focus off God, we creates a space that the devil can use against us, which will totally evaporates our faith resulting in us denying the hope of God. The only fear that should be controlling our lives is the fear of God. Our life span here on earth is to live a successful Christian life in Christ so we can experience all the peace that comes from fearing God, for there is no want to them who fear God (Ps. 34:9; 2 Sam. 23:2–3).

The fear of God brings everlasting joy; the fear of the Spirit results in destruction.

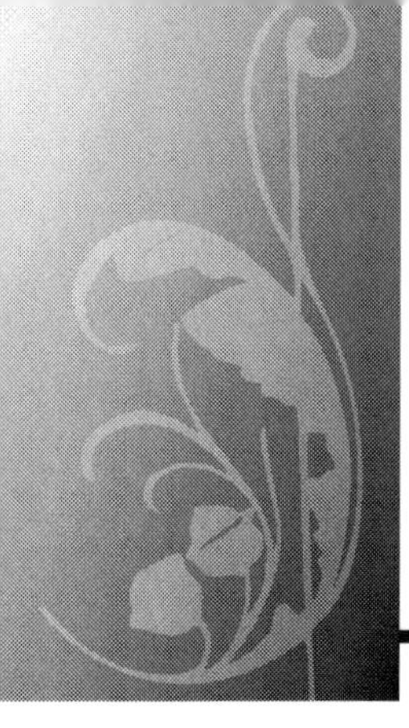

Anger, a Destructive Emotion

Anger is mankind's deadliest emotion. If not channeled in the proper manner, it can destroy their entire lives. Anger is natural, but when taken out of context, it can be an unjust and uncontrolled emotion. This spirit of anger can destroy a person physically, mentally, and, most of all, spiritually. Therefore, we must be alert to the signs and resolve the situation sooner rather than later before it escalates out of control. Anger in of itself is not a sin. However, it can easily become a sin if it is not put in its proper content, Thus, the Word of God admonishes us "be angry and sin not; let not the sun go down upon our anger." Anger, like everything we do, boils down to our choice. In the Bible, there are two different type of anger. The righteous anger, which is of God and is demonstrated in forbearance and patience, and the anger of the spirit, which is a manifestation of the flesh and is manipulated by Satan (Eph. 4:26).

God is holy and righteous. Thus he cannot sin.The anger of God is always justified and is based on His principles, upholding the truth when responding to mankind's disobedience to Him. God's anger is an aspect of His divine characters, love, righteousness, and His hatred towards sin, His anger is geared at persons who violate His holy Word. God is gracious and slow to anger. He is abounding in love, forgiveness, and justice. Thus still he has a great displeasure of sin, showing His disapproval to all unrighteousness and injustice, His anger is directed to those who come between His relationship with His children. God expresses righteous anger, to put an end to evil and the suffering of His people while bringing others into the knowledge of Him. His anger is merciful even when we hurt Him, yet because of His love, His anger is just for a moment, and His favor is for a lifetime (Ps. 30:5).

God's love is incomprehensible toward us, and so is His anger/wrath in the displeasure of sin, for the scriptures tells us, "For the wrath of God is revealed from heaven against all ungodliness and unrighteousness of man." His anger is always under control and is an attribute of his wisdom and justice. His anger is unchanging toward sin.

The Old Testament illustrations many of God's righteous anger. Most notable one is the flood of Noah's generation, His wrath was revealed on the uncleanliness and vile passion of mankind. Just as in Noah's time, Jesus Christ is going to pour out His wrath on this present world at His second coming to earth, but not by flood, His judgment will be hellfire. God's anger is in defense to His holiness and love. He sent His Son Jesus Christ to the cross to endure the pains of mankind's sins so we can escape His future wrath. As a result of Christ sufferings on the cross, he was given the responsibility from God to judge the world and to pour out His wrath on those who rejected Him (Rev. 5:7, 6–17; John 3:36).

Righteous anger expresses godly qualities such as long-suffering, patience, and meekness so we can make peace with others rather than tearing them down, turning our anger into love, thinking of what God would do in our situation. It's based on our love for God and others, showing godly concern and a sorrow-filled heart over the things of God that are being distorted, misrepresented, and watered down in this world. Righteous anger is a godlike anger. It is consistent with the holy and righteous characteristics of Christ, for it is based on man's violation of God's laws. It's not explosive, instead it's compassionate and gracious, but, most of all, patient toward others. Our righteous anger represents our faith in God, and is controlled by the Holy Spirit living in us, we defend God intensively, doing it in a godly and virtuous way (Rom. 12:19).

Righteous anger must always reflect Christ in our actions, turning evil that befalls us into good by demonstrating humility and selflessness, faith and love, thereby allowing that evil to become our testimony by us showing love. In responding to anger, our defense must have the tendencies of love, gentleness, respect, and a good conscience always showing good behavior. Righteous anger does not lose temper. It always seeks to do good, remains calm, restrains our emotions and exhibits self-control which prohibits us for sinning as we hold fast to the truth of the Word.

Righteous anger must be compatible with God's nature adopting to the teachings of the apostle James as he admonishes us "to be quick to listen and slow to speak." Mindful not to grieve the Holy Spirit, not focusing on the personal offenses instead, we respond in a controlled way displaying righteous anger, for we don't take pleasure in the judgment of mankind (Ps. 78:38; Eph. 4:27).

The spirit of anger, which Satan masterminds, is a joy killer, a communication dampener that tears apart mankind's relationship with God and others, for it's a very destructive, unhealthy emotion that comes with serious consequences. This type of anger becomes a sin when its desire and motivation take vengeance and cause bodily harm, this anger is formed as a result of pride or selfishness, an expression of hatred or malice. It is a product of mankind's sin nature, which is placed in the mind of a person and being instigated by Satan, this emotion destroys others. And it drives someone to do the unthinkable without properly thinking of other solutions. The devil uses this destructive emotion to make people feel as if they are in charge and to sin against God themselves without having any regards for the person to whom they are inflecting the pain against. Anger of the spirit is produced by the flesh and demonstrates unrighteousness, where there is no self-control or patience, which leads to rebellion against God and man, it only seeks to please self (James 1:20).

The Bible tells that such anger was present at the beginning of time, as was told in the story of the first sons of Adam and Eve, Cain and Abel. Cain allowed the spirit of anger and jealousy of his brother to get out of control, where he could not constrain his thoughts and anger, which resulted in the killing of his brother. Although God warned Cain about the destructive power of sin, he gave into his sin, as it was rooted in the spirit of pride. Cain's anger showed his lack of godliness and godly character, and he demonstrated the sinful nature of his carnal mind because of his resentment towards God and Abel. God knew the heart of Cain. He asked Cain why he was wrong/angry, God was trying to help Cain have a change of heart towards his brother. Yet Cain refused to listen to God. He allowed Satan and his anger to take control of him as he committed such sin and evil against his brother Abel. After Cain killed his brother, he did not show any remorse. neither did he repent of his sins. God judged Cain and placed a curse on his life. After which, Cain decided to separate himself from God (Genesis 4:4–8,16).

Sinful anger is dominated by the desires of the flesh, the eyes, and the pride of life. And it is planted in the hearts of mankind, which energizes them to sin against God, the Word of God tells us, "Sinful anger can never make things right with God." Sinful anger does not produce righteousness. Instead, it promotes unrighteousness, which prompts persons to act passively and alienates one from God as it leads to selfishness and arrogance. This anger violates the spirit of God. It takes a person's emotion and spiritual life far away from God. It allows the spirit of anger to make mankind act unjustly, bringing them down to the level of a fool. Thus, the Bible tells us, "Be not quick in your spirit to become angry for anger lodges in the hearts of fools." When the spirit of anger is displayed in our lives by our choices and actions, the devil takes full advantage of the given situation, as our behavior reflecting the tendency that mankind is ready to commit sin. Satan encourages the spirit of anger to make us sin, by triggering different emotions within such as jealousy, bitterness, and malice, making mankind a slave to sin which result in bringing dishonor to themselves and those in their lives (Eccl. 7:9).

It is important to note that the spirit of anger led the religious leaders and people to crucify Jesus Christ on the cross, they were angry at Him because of His teachings, especially when he declared Himself to be the Son of God. They also had the spirit of anger and jealousy in their hearts, as they marveled at His knowledge, wisdom and abilities to perform miracles. They said his powers came from Satan.

The religious leaders were mostly angry at Jesus because he was a threat to their religious system and their way of life. They had no ungodly or unrighteous motive for killing Jesus, it was all about pride, hypocrisy, and arrogance, which was instigated by Satan, inflaming in their hearts hatred, ignorance, and unbelief. By them killing Jesus, they believed he deserved their judgement. Thus they took matters into their own hands; however, what they wanted to happen didn't because on the third day, Jesus Christ rose proving to the religious leaders that he was in fact who he claimed to be, the Son of God. This should be a lesson that mankind must learn, anger only enslaves us to sin, giving us temporary satisfaction to our sin nature and the flesh. (Luke 23:34).

To defeat the spirit of anger, first mankind must admit to the anger issues in their lives. Recognizing, and accepting there is a problem which needs to be remedied then begin to deal with it immediately by confessing their anger unto God, in genuine repentance and prayers. God will help them by destroying the spirit of anger and replace it with the fruits of His spirit, formulating His principles in their lives, as they adopt biblical strategies such as being quick to listen and slow to speak; for a soft word turns away anger. Thus developing the art of self-control and successfully defeat the spirit of anger (Prov. 19:11).

The key to overcoming the spirit of anger is learning self-control. Self-control is a form of self-discipline, self-restraint and godly behavior in our actions. Self-control is one of the gifts of fruits of the spirit, which is produced by the Holy Spirit of God, it's the embodiment of humility. Ignoring petty disagreements, resolving disagreements immediately, offering forgiveness, refraining from evil words, and not associating yourself with angry people. Thus, making no provisions for the flesh nor allow the spirit of anger to enter our lives. Our self-control is a product of our faith and our relationship with Christ, growing in the manifestation of His godly qualities, His characters, and filled in the knowledge of Word (Titus 2:6; 2 Peter 1:6).

In exhibiting self-control, we are obedient to God, having sound judgment in our conducts being bounded by the laws of God, as it helps us to incorporate all aspects of the fruit of the spirit. Not allowing anger to consume us, practicing empathy, compassion, kindness, staying calm, ruling our thoughts, and attitudes in all situations, for the Bible tells us that vengeance belongs to God. Therefore, in our development and growth in self-control, we become stronger than any strong man, as God is with us in our battles, encouraging us not give into the spirit of anger (Prov. 14:29; Titus 2:12).

Nehemiah was to be governor of Judah and he wanted to rebuild the wall of Jerusalem which had broken down. He was faced with many obstacles in his path when building the wall of Jerusalem. Despite all the opposition he received, he always demonstrated righteous anger throughout, as a result, he used his righteous anger to bring change to the people of Israel. When faced with opposition, instead of displaying anger, Nehemiah lifted his voice in prayer to God, being steadfast in his faith, for he knew God was sovereign in the situation he was facing. He displayed righteous anger before he acted, by consulting with himself and getting his anger under control. He sought God's wisdom and then took action by demonstrating self-control when confronting his enemies using biblical principles to resolve the problem. He trusted in God and guarded his heart against selfish ambitions, motives, and thoughts, thus vigilantly watching his enemies as he put his heart into his work, leaving no room for Satan.

Nehemiah expressed anger by demonstrating and setting an example of godliness, for he listened to the people, thus laying aside his rights and not giving into his powers because he feared God. Hence, he was committed to God and his work, for he knew that he would be accountable for his actions so he did not disobey God's Word (Neh. 4:15, 5:6–13).

All mankind, both Christians and non-Christians, can learn from Nehemiah, he demonstrated courage, wisdom, perseverance and prayer when dealing with his anger. He gave serious thought to the situation he was facing before he acted upon them, he knew responding in anger would be following the desires of the flesh and Satan. Thus he submit the conflicts unto God, learned to resolve problems biblically, creating a personal guidelines to remember that anger is a scheme of Satan and is spiritual. The lesson for mankind is; don't deal with the spirit of anger in our own self, fight it in the power of the Holy Spirit by allowing God to direct our minds (Eph. 4:26–27).

As followers of Christ, when the spirit of anger comes upon us, we approach it in the love of Christ, compassion, and mending conflict, and not yielding to our emotions. Walking in the fear of God, putting aside all anger, malice, and abusive speech from our mouth and adorn ourselves in godly behavior, as the scriptures says, "The discretion of a man deferreth his anger and it is his glory to pass over a transgression." Therefore, marked our hearts with compassion and love (Prov. 19:11).

Refuse to allow the spirit of anger to paralyze your destiny in Christ.

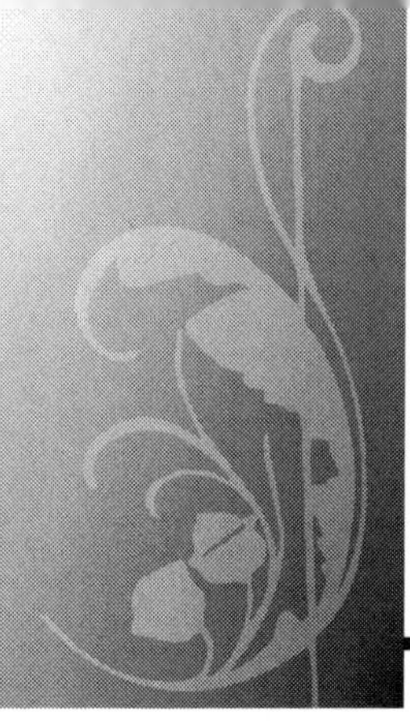

The Gift of Forgiveness

Forgiving is a command from God that he emphasizes strongly in the last six commandments of the Ten Commandments. It is a conscience choice, an act of self where we give over all our hurts and pain to God. Forgiveness is biblical, a spiritual function, and it is life's most important gift. It is an act of obedience and submission to God's will. It's a decision and an act of our will to release someone from his or her guilt and ourselves from the pain and sufferings.

Forgiveness is the same as love, it is unconditional. It is not only practical but possible, it is beneficial to all parties involved because it's all about reconciliation with the person who hurt you. Forgiveness is mostly important because it strengthens our relationship with God for the scriptures tells us, "If we forgive others their sin, God will forgive us." Forgiveness begins and ends in our hearts. It is an emotion and is our sole responsibility, whether we are the offender or not, which then will lead to joy and peace of mind (Matt. 6:14).

Forgiveness is one of the strong pillow of the Christian faith, and it's important to God because he looks at our relationship with one another and measure the level of our obedience to Him. Forgiveness is demonstrated in two ways–either receiving or extending. True forgiveness happens when pride is out of our hearts, it is unconditional, and cannot be rushed, it takes time and courage which cannot be separated.

With forgiveness, we display love and mercy required of God, freeing each party emotionally and spiritually from the bondage of sin, as our eternal destiny depends on our willingness to forgive. Jesus grants us the power to forgive each other just as he has forgiven us, for it is in our best interest to receive the blessings of God (Luke 6:37).

Our love and obedience towards God leads to forgiveness. It's not just about our feelings, it's all for God and us obtaining a right standing with Him as our faith leads us to extend forgiveness. Forgiveness and love goes together. They show us how to be compassionate, loving, and in conjunction with what the Word of God commands for us to be—kind, tenderhearted, and forgiving to one another. Therefore, in having the love of God dwelling in our hearts, it helps us to be kindhearted and always ready to forgive, and not allowing the flesh and the spirit of un-forgiveness to engulf our lives.

These two characters of Christ, forgiveness and love are powerful witnesses of God, which places us in a different category from the people of this world. As the world witness our forgiveness and reconciliation of those who wrong us or whom we wrong, it portrays a strong message of the power of forgiveness and the power of God (Eph. 4:32).

To understand true forgiveness, we must look at it from God's perspective. His act of pure grace, promoted by His love and mercy, His decision of forgiveness to restore life to mankind. Although God's forgiveness was costly to Him, he went forward with it by sacrificing His only beloved Son. God's forgiveness was given to mankind. Although we didn't deserve His forgiveness, it's by His grace and favor that he forgave all our sins, wiping our slate clean. That is the true definition of genuine forgiveness and love. The perfect example of forgiveness, which all mankind should imitate and not hold any grudges or remorse towards other fellow man.

Like God the Father, Jesus Christ demonstrated another perfect example of forgiveness as he hung on the cross at Calvary, after all the sufferings he endured from those who crucified Him. Yet on the cross, he prayed for them saying, "Father forgive them for they know not what they do." By Jesus praying for forgiveness of His killers, mankind saw His heart and His true nature, and it encourages us to open our hearts to the forgiveness which he provided so we can extend that same measure of forgiveness towards others (Luke 23:34; Ps. 103:12).

For mankind to receive the forgiveness from God, we must humble ourselves before Him and in all honesty, confess our sins by faith, clearing the guilt that was the barrier between us and God. Acknowledge our failures to Him, repent wholeheartedly, and receive His forgiveness in faith, believing that God has forgiven our sins and trusting that he will bring emotional healing to our lives. Appreciating the fullness of His gift of forgiveness.

There is an inseparable link between receiving God's forgiveness and our willingness to forgive others. We ought to forgive just as God forgave us because our eternal destiny depends on our willingness to forgive. Hence, upon coming to faith in Christ Jesus, we become a new person. Thereby we must have the same characters of Christ of which include forgiveness, this is a crucial process in experiencing true peace and the peace of God (Rom. 12:18; Ps. 32:1–5).

Forgiveness is necessary in living a successful Christian life. Therefore in extending forgiveness, we must first acknowledge the wrong that the individual has done, then proceed by going to him or her privately and address the hurt that he or she has caused. From the heart, verbally forgive the person whether he or she shows remorse for their actions or not. By doing this, lives will be restored, feeling spiritually free, as we experience healing emotionally and mentally. Forgive in love because forgiveness is not based on his or her actions of whether to accept it, but our desires to please God and His command to love our enemies. We are to do good to those who hate us because love and forgiveness cannot be separated.

In choosing to forgive, we knowingly relinquish our rights of getting even, by praying for those who hurt us with genuine concern for their eternal salvation now that we have bestowed forgiveness to them. Forgiving others leads to spiritual maturity and growth, taking away pride and un-forgiveness completely out of our hearts, as forgiveness brings humility, healing and reconciliation. After extending forgiveness, we must not hold on the past hurt, instead, ask God's help to forget it and remember it no more, thus moving forward in our faith with our minds focused on Him (Luke 6:27:18:15-17).

As humans, it can be very challenging to forget. However, if we continue to remember our hurt, that could be a sign that we have not genuinely forgiven that person. Hence, after extending forgiveness, we ought to forget because forgiving and forgetting are both choices of the heart, and are vital components for genuine reconciliation, therefore forgetting is choosing life and happiness, refusing to be bogged down with unhealthy memories. God's forgiveness is unconditional, and when he forgave us of our sins, he remembers them no more. Also we His followers should adopt that same principle of forgiveness by also forgetting (Phil. 3:13).

Another aspect of forgiveness is receiving forgiveness and reconciliation with those we offended. This is also important because Jesus Himself tells us " If thy brother hath ought against thee; go be reconciled to thy brothers" Before we can offer anything unto God, if we offend anyone, seek their forgiveness and be reconciled with them. This type of forgiveness focuses on the offended person and not ourselves, for it's our responsibility to make things right and preserve Christian love and peace with one another. This might be one of the most difficult thing a person must do, however, it is a requirement from Jesus Christ before he could accept our offerings. To accomplish this task, we must do away with our pride, accepting that it's our responsibility to amends, and pray to God for His strength to achieve this mission and to softening of the hearts of the offended to grant us their forgiveness.

In approaching our offender, we must be humble before them, speaking to him or her in private, genuinely acknowledging our wrongdoings, and asking for their forgiveness. It is that person's obligation on how they respond to our request, should that person choose to rebuke us before offering forgiveness, it is his or her biblical right to do so. However, it is apparent that this forgiveness between both parties takes place, for without it, we would not be rendered fit to commune with God (Matt. 5:23–24).

Seeking forgiveness is our responsibility. Reconciliation depends on the offender. This is why God commanded forgiveness and reconciliation, which is to admonish us His followers not to be angry with our fellowman, but rather be in true unity and love with each other. We cannot worship God if we have a heart of unforgiveness because our worship becomes ineffective.

Reconciling demonstrates our obedience, displaying humility by not allowing our self-pride to overshadow us, it shows the quality of our love for God, others, and our dedication to following the commands of God.

Thus, we mature more spiritually and have greater self-control over our actions, being mindful of our relationship with others. This process of forgiveness purifies our spirits, hearts, and minds, where we now have a clear conscience on what is required before we can have complete communication with God in prayer (Rom. 12:18).

Receiving and seeking forgiveness plays a vital role in being a fulfilled Christian and living for God. However, self-forgiveness is also vital for living a productive filled life and not self-hating ourselves living in misery. Self-forgiveness is an obstacle that deceives people in thinking they are not worthy of God's forgiveness. This is a trick of the Devil, which is the spirit of deception, for he wants people to believe that their past sins are so terrible that God cannot forgive them. That is a lie, once we honestly confess and repent of our sins before God, he instantly forgives us and remembers them no more. Satan does not want mankind to know that when God forgives, he does not hold that sin against them anymore, Satan puts those sins into our minds for us to continually feel guilty. The Bible never mentioned self-forgiveness for the mere reason that "mankind cannot forgive themselves of their sins." Only God can forgive sins. Hence, because of God's forgiveness, we realize that God has already forgiven those sins we've committed in the past. However, there is no need to feel guilty or unworthy of His gift of forgiveness (Phil. 4:8–9).

Self-forgiveness is important for the releasing and overcoming of one's guilt, so he or she can be able to forgive others. It is a personal choice and our willingness to denounce guilt and self-pride from controlling our minds, for the scriptures tells us, "Pride goes before destruction and a haughty spirit before a fall." In holding on to guilt and self-pride will only lead to destruction.

Self-forgiveness comes down to our self-will and our action to change the direction of our lives, by taking the first step which is trusting in Jesus Christ and His redemptive power of His forgiveness and move forward with Him, taking solace in the fact that he has already forgiven us. Strengthened and courageous in God rather than giving in to our own negative thoughts and becoming a victims of self-guilt.

God forgives all our sins, no matter how small or great they may be. If we asked of Him, believing and accepting His gift of forgiveness in faith and allowing the power of the Holy Spirit to heal us from within so we could appreciate our own self-worth and let our light shine and God be glorified. If a person chooses not to let go of the sins which God has already forgiven him or her of, then that person has elevated their standards higher than those of God's. Mankind needs to recognize and realize that, if God has forgiven them, then the highest judge in the whole universe has already forgiven them. When God forgives, His verdict is final and he revisits it no more. Henceforth, mankind should stop thinking on their past sins, but strive to live in the life of God's forgiveness (Prov. 16:18).

Unforgiveness is direct disobedience to God's command. It is in violation of His Word. Therefore receiving His grace, which leads to salvation would be impossible for anyone with an unforgiving spirit. Unforgiveness is choosing not to forgive others, a direct command from God. Thus, it blocks God's presence from entering lives, unforgiveness is incompatible with the standards of being a follower of Christ because the scriptures tells us that God is a forgiving God.

Refusing to forgive is a result of pride, conceit, and self-justification. It is being justified in one's own arrogance, which only shows that they don't have personal love for God, for the Scriptures tells us, "He that do not love me does not keep my sayings." Unforgiveness keeps us in a dark place in life, for it cuts us off from God and our healing emotionally and mentally, it is rooted in bitterness, anger, and hatred, thus alienating people from God and bringing them closer to Satan. It also affects relationships in one's life, specifically their prayer life with God. God would not answer their prayers, if there is any animosity or bitterness in their hearts, thus, he admonishes us to be reconciled with those who have offended us (Mark 11:25; John 14:24).

In the Bible, the story of Joseph is a great story of forgiveness. Joseph demonstrated genuine forgiveness and love for God and his brothers, although his older brothers sold him into slavery and he was taken into Egypt. Joseph was favored and loved more by their father, and this was known to his brothers, who hated him. However, what made them hate him more was when Joseph told his brothers about the dreams he had. They interpreted the dream and asked Joseph if he would reign over them, and they hated him even more. And as a result, they sold him at the tender age of seventeen.

Joseph's dream was a vision of God's plan for his life, so God was with him as he grew in the confidence and strength of God. He prospered even through all his suffering and circumstances encountered in the land of Egypt. He remained faithful unto God. Joseph was sent to prison falsely for a crime he did not commit. Yet, he remained faithful to God, for he feared God. While in prison, he interpreted the dreams of two prisoners, and his interpretation of their dreams came to pass (Gen. 37:5–28).

While still in prison, Pharaoh had a troubling dream. No one in his kingdom could interpret his dream. The prisoner whose dream Joseph interpreted remembered him and told Pharaoh of him. Joseph interpreted Pharaoh's dream, informing him that there would be seven years of plenty and seven years of famine in the land.

Pharaoh heeded to Joseph's words and stored up food during the seven years of plenty. Pharaoh then promoted Joseph as governor, second-in-command in the land of Egypt. During the seven years of famine, only Egypt had food, and Joseph was in charge of selling the food. Joseph's brothers came from Canaan to purchase food. Immediately, Joseph recognized them. However, the brothers did not know it was him, for Joseph was dressed in his Egyptian royal attire. Thus, the fulfillment of his dream. he was ruler, not only of Egypt, but of his brothers.

Still unknown to his brothers, Joseph gave them several tests to see if they had changed. And when Joseph recognized that his brothers were remorseful and made acknowledged their guilt, he was overcome with emotions. Then he revealed himself to his brothers, saying to them, "I am Joseph. Is my father still alive?" The brothers began to fear him because of their guilt (Gen. 42–44).

Joseph forgave his brothers in his heart a long time ago, for he realized that God planned for him to be in Egypt to save his people. He demonstrated love, forgiveness, and reconciliation towards his brothers when they showed real repentance. Rather than seeking revenge on his brothers, Joseph forgave them, thus telling them, "You sold me here, but God sent me before you to preserve life. So do not to be angry with yourselves." And they all wept.

Joseph's faith in God enabled him to forgive his brothers and not hold them accountable, he demonstrating genuine forgiveness and Christ likeness. In everything he still remained loyal and faithful to God, thereby he brought honor and glory to God. Joseph recognized God's favor and presence in his life from a young age, and maintained his integrity, by remaining humble, loyal, and faithful, for he was totally dependent on God. He never allowed bitterness and revenge to hinder the purpose of God in his life (Gen. 45).

Joseph's forgiveness was of hope and encouragement as he showed his brothers love and compassion. Thus starting the healing and reconciliation process. The healing and reconciliation phase of forgiveness cannot start unless the offender shows genuine remorse. Therefore, as followers of Christ, we can learn from Joseph that genuine forgiveness is a choice, an act of one's will, which leads to healing and releasing the debt caused by others. It is not overlooking their sins. It's surrendering our rights and reconciling relationships, and being able to forgive. replacing our anger with love.

Forgiveness is like love. They always seek the best in others. It's a choice that we make within our hearts, with the Holy Spirit within us, it makes it easier for us to forgive because we are now in a relationship with Christ (Matt. 6:12).

Forgiveness must be done sooner rather than later; repentance and forgiveness are essential for genuine reconciliation.

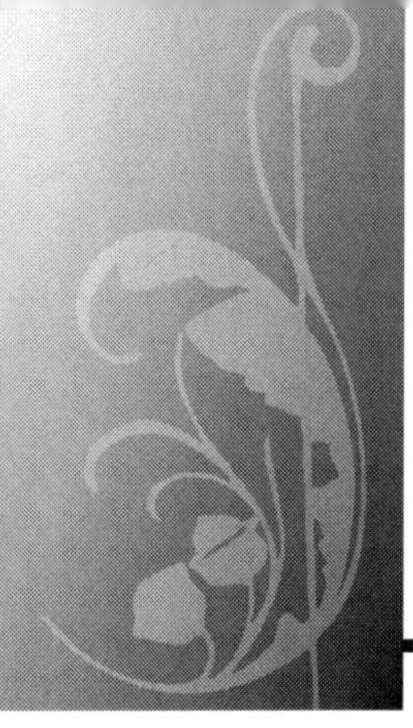

A Fulfilled Life with God

A fulfilled life with God is our allegiance and commitment to the one true, living, and sovereign God. Keeping and adhering to His commandments, being faithful to His supreme authority in our lives. Having strong determination to serve and be of service to Him, standing firm in the gospel as he becomes the head and controller of our lives. Basing all our priorities on Him. His Word and daily fellowship. Hiding His Word in our hearts, minds, and souls; live according to its teachings and commands; and abiding in God's love, fulfilling our purpose in Christ of being fruitful by sharing the gospel of truth and producing new fruits. Living with integrity, having a good reputation, and walking in the ways of God, thus becoming an example and a witness for both believers and unbelievers, as we shine the light and love of Christ in this evil world (Ex. 20; John 15:1–6).

Faithfulness is one of the attributes of living a fulfilled life with God, as we look to our source of life, Jesus Christ, seeking His kingdom and righteousness as His Word admonishes us, "Seek first the kingdom of God and His righteousness and all things shall be added unto you." For only in Jesus Christ can we have a fulfilled life. We learn how to be spiritually disciplined, endeavoring to be like Him, thereby remain connected with Him in our continuous prayer and worship time, which makes us wise and aware of His ever-present presence, thereby filling us with joy and happiness. Expressing our God-given purpose in our actions and making a difference in the world while moving forward with matters that concern God being focused on what he has called us to do rather than ourselves. Walking bountifully in humility, and being faithful to the service of God, trusting and yielding to the Holy Spirit. Focusing on those in need and dedicate ourselves to them by being compassionate and nurturing them physically, mentally, and most importantly, spiritually (Matt. 6:33).

In living a fulfilled life in Christ, we share our life experiences, encouraging and helping to develop and be a positive influence to others in their Christian walk so they can mature spiritually and be a blessing in the body of Christ. Enriching, empowering, and impacting lives for God demonstrating to them on how to live a life that is characterized by God's love and is exhibited in good conduct and godly behaviors. As fulfilled followers living for Christ, we love and enjoy doing the work of Christ, for it is our earthly purpose, passion and mission to be a witness for Him, which in turn gives us on ending joy. We have our hearts filled with genuine love for Him, with a deep sense of peace and fulfillment within us. A life of fulfillment can only be found in the saving grace of God through His son Jesus Christ, giving our lives totally over to Him, thereby working together with Christ to achieve His ordained purpose as we submit to His leadership in our lives (Gal. 5:22).

A fulfilled life with Christ consists of us not being subjected to the things of the world, the world is trying to discredit the credibility the Word of God by making right what God's Word vividly say is wrong. Hence, we do not partake in such. Instead, we remain committed to God's Word, the true and living Word, its commands, teachings and values, no matter the cost. We as followers of Christ live in the world, but are not of the world, remaining committed to God in both good and bad times. Entrusting our lives totally to God's care, being strengthened by Him, committed to be faithful to Him in all things and allowing the Holy Spirit to fill us with the peace of God. Thus, we are not moved nor enticed by the workings or trends of what is going on in the world.

Instead, we remain fulfilled in Christ and remaining steadfast towards Him, accepting His Word to be the truth and not being shaken by what is going on around us, for we know we have a greater calling in heaven. Knowing that the things of this world are temporal and vanity. Nothing of value, as they only bring joy for a season, a time and will pass away along with this world. Therefore, as Christ followers, we find no joy and no fulfillment in this world, as a result, we place all our focus, time and energy in the things of God, which are everlasting and eternally binding (John 17:16).

In every work that we His followers do here on earth for Christ, we are storing up treasures in heaven, for God will reward us for our service to Him because our life on earth is based on what we do for God. A living sacrifice unto the Lord is what our lives should be, holy and acceptable. The instruments of righteousness which brings glory and honor to God. Therefore, our work and times are important here on earth, because they are counted in eternity. Hence there is no limitation to our abilities in Christ.

Jesus Christ lived a fulfilled life here on earth, and we His followers must be imitators of that life, following His examples so we can be found in Him, by allowing it to become our lifetime goal, being motivated in doing everything unto Christ, for we know there is no comparison between serving God and being of this world. They are very different. Evil fills the world. Everlasting joy, peace, and happiness is found in God, a true fulfilled life can only be found in Christ Jesus. Hence, we worry not about our own lives, as the apostle Paul says, "I am crucified with Christ nevertheless I live; yet not I, but Christ lives in me." Our lives are all about Jesus Christ (Gal. 2:20).

We are fulfilled in Christ, being comforted by His grace, offering up praises, and reverencing Him, he then guides our every steps, helping us to live righteously, morally and to stay on the straight and narrow path. Living up to His righteous standards, placing a significant value on our calling. Striving to accomplish it for the glorification of Christ, continuing to renew our minds in the things of God so we can be more of an influence to mankind endeavoring to change their minds from this evil world towards Jesus Christ (John 10:27).

A fulfilled life with Christ allows us to be content with the blessings that God has given to us, no matter the size, for it sustains and keeps us. Thus, we learn always how to give thanks in all things whether great or small, being satisfied with them because godliness with contentment is great gain according to the Word of God. We have the priority of godliness that stems from a close relationship with Christ, which is more valuable than any amount of wealth. Hence, we find all fulfillment, joy, and perspective of eternal gain because our earthly gains are all temporal and will not bring true joy. God has called us His followers to a life marked by contentment so we do not lose His promises regarding eternity. Therefore, in living a fulfilled in Christ is to live a contented life, it helps us to more focused on God, thus giving us strength as we become energetic unto good work and honoring and pleasing God in our lives. We live high above our lives' circumstances, thereby taking no pleasure in our infirmities, needs, or distresses, but rather taking pleasure in the power of God, relying on His provisions, and promises (1 Thess. 5:18; 1 Tim. 6:6).

Jesus Christ lived a fulfilled life while on earth, and he was the epitome of faithfulness and contentment. He was obedient. He learned it and was submissive to His Father. He trusted God, so His desires were only towards the will of His Father. The Word tells us, "Jesus had to learn obedience by the things which he suffered." Yet he remained faithful and fulfilled, even unto the every end.

Therefore, as followers of Christ, the more we remain obedient, faithful, and knowing of God's purpose for our lives, the more meaningful and fulfilling our lives become as we strive to accomplish His plans, thus being productive here on earth. We know a fulfilled life in Christ is not merely subjected to the joy and peace of mind received on earth but also in heaven, being identified with Christ and things eternal (John 4:36; Heb. 5:8).

Therefore, as we remain fulfilled in our lives with God, our minds and hearts remains transformed with His Word, teachings, and laws. We love and appreciate Him even more, being filled with the knowledge that it's not through our good works we are blessed, but by accepting, fearing, serving, and being faithful to the Almighty God. Confident in the sovereignty and supremacy of Christ, looking forward to His coming and being mindful never to neglect His Word, commands, and instructions, but to continue living a fulfilled godly life that brings honor to God. Humbling ourselves before God, desiring only to please Him, living in a holy and godly manner, abiding and depending on God, the source of our joy which infiltrates our every thoughts, senses and behaviors. As we allow our lives to shine, be visible, and become an evidence of what a fulfilled life in God represents so others can see and want to experience such peace, joy and fulfillment too in their lives, thus producing new fruits for the kingdom of God (Phil. 2:2).

Trusting in God, serving others is the key to living a life of fulfillment with God.

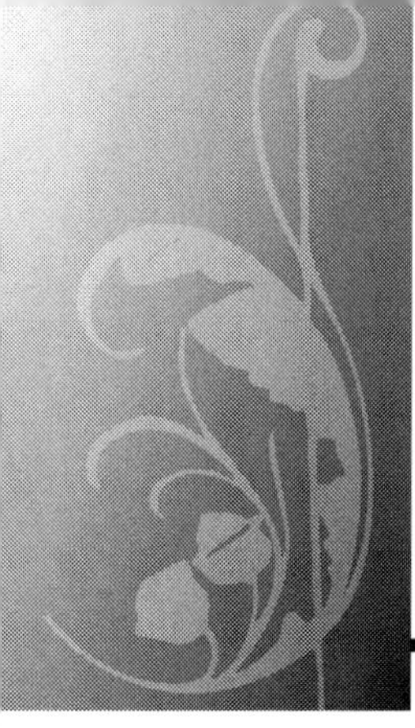

Building a Godly Home

The family is the most fundamental aspect of human existence and the basic building block of mankind. God created the institute of family and a godly home in the garden of Eden when he made woman, a helper and companion for Adam, when he realized that it was not good for man to be alone. God designed the union of marriage to be a blessing to mankind, thus he placed a high priority on marriage and family as he told Adam and Eve to be fruitful and multiply on earth.

The marriage of Adam and Eve was an earthly picture of the spiritual union between Christ and the church, which results as a joining of one genuine love for another, the subjection of the church to Christ, and the producing of offspring, which are the principles that we must follow to be a spiritually strong family. The family was designed as the first source of spiritual preparation and training for life. It should inspire and motivate us to be spiritually productive for God. It is the channel of His blessings and revelation where we can be spiritually matured (Gen. 2:18,24).

Therefore, in building a godly home, it must consist of a husband and a wife who have genuine love for each other, basing on their love for God. A family that is surrounded by love and is magnified in their holiness growing in godliness and the giving of affection towards one another. Thus they are able to correct and instruct each other when necessary. For a godly home to function properly, it must be built on the foundation of Christ so Satan cannot penetrate it as he did in the garden of Eden.

It's important that the husband and wife focus on their different roles in the home and carry out their individual duties as God commanded. The family must be separated from the world and focused solely on

God's method of a family so they would be able to have a joyous, productive, protected, and faithful union. Strong and steadfast in the faith, demonstrating the humility of God, and laying strong, godly fundamentals by allowing God to lead, protect, and guide each member of the family. Making sure that their relationship with God is in absolute good standing, both internally and externally, so the world can witness the beauty of godly home that is centered in the teachings of the gospel of Christ (1 Cor. 16:13–14).

In building a godly home, we first must be obedient to God and making Him the ultimate head of the home. Revere His lordship as head in our prayers, which in turn creates a solid and strong foundation in the home as the presence of God is felt in the family and throughout the entire home. We enjoy His presence in our prayers, song worship, and Bible reading on a daily basis, thereby the family developing a faith-based relationship with God starting from the home. Without God, our efforts of a godly home will be futile. Thus the psalmist tells us, "Except the Lord build the home, we labor in vain."

As a Christian family we ought to make God our primary focus, as it's our responsibility to build a godly home that is grounded in the things of God and His Word, being mindful not to base our lives on superficial and materialistic things, but instead be consumed with the characteristics and things of God. Becoming a family with a godly mind-set that has the burning fire of God in their hearts, fascinated with Him every moment of our lives as he becomes the life of the home and our lives. Nothing can be more satisfying and rewarding in a family, and brings such peace, joy, love, and unity within the home other than Jesus Christ (Matt. 7:24–27; Ps. 127:1).

In striving to build a godly home, our faith in God must be strong as we partner up with God to protect the home from destructive spiritual influences, therefore we the parents must be very vigilant as to what we allow in our homes. The home must demonstrate godly characters such as humility, compassion, patience, and willingness to forgive, but must importantly, have the virtue of love that binds families together in unity and complete dedication to the family.

To be godly parents, our lives should always depict that of Christ being spiritually and rationally inclined, creating the strong presence of

God in our hearts which is then protruded throughout the home with the help of the Holy Spirit. Sin begins in the mind. Therefore, we must diligently guard the eyes and ears of our family by being selective as to what is seen or listened to in the homes, whether through television, the Internet, and books. We must be on guard so the mind is not corrupted and does not dishonor God and the values of the home (Col. 3:12).

In the family, biblical respect and communication are valued highly and shown to everyone in the home, which leads to total obedience to God in our hearts and providing unconditional love, moral purity, honesty, and trust within the family. We uphold biblical principles as each member of the family has understanding of the importance of fulfilling his or her God-given roles in the home. Showing respect to each other by giving up their own needs and desires. Hence, adhering to God's biblical teaching on the family, creating quality family time to spend together, reading and studying the Word of God as a family, thus strengthening and reinforcing good godly family values in the home, growing spiritually, rationally, and emotionally and building a happy and healthy home life.

In following God's blueprint that the Bible provided for the family, it will lead to growth in each individual relationship with God, creating closeness, comfort, and genuine love in the family. As humility and mutual submission fills the home whereby others can see the righteousness of God through them by their devotion to each other, the children, and God (1 Peter 2:17).

Jesus' life was characterized as compassionate, merciful, kind, caring, honest, and peaceable, for he was obedient and submissive to both His heavenly Father and earthly parents, because he was focus and serious-minded about His life mission on earth. Thus he became a servant, and no selfishness was found in Him. That being said, in maintaining a godly home, we must remember that God is the head of the home and everything we do must reflect His characteristics of which submission is vital in sustaining a happy home once the guideline is being followed and respected. Firstly, God as the head of the home, then the husband, followed by the wife and children. Submission is for all individuals in the family. A husband is subjected to God. Husbands loves their wives. Wives are submissive to their husband with love, and children obey and honor their parents. This is God's blueprint for the family. It does not deal with superiority nor inferiority, for we are all equal to God. But instead it refers to husband and wife as joint heirs in the building and running of family (Luke 2:51).

In the sight of God, man and woman are both spiritually equal and equally united to Him, for we are all one in Christ Jesus. God is the head of every man, for we were created in the image and likeness of Him. We are all sinners in need of His grace and salvation. Men and women were divinely designed to complement each other, for they both jointly share in having dominion over the created beings, along with the upbringing of their children. They both are equal, respectively, having equal duties unto each other. Therefore the wife is not inferior to the husband. She was created for him.

Both husband and wife have different roles to play in order to make the family strive and be a blessing to God, although the husband is the spiritual leader of the home, it imperative that he imitates Christ, thus desiring to fulfill their divine and holy calling as the leader of the family by having a strong and intimate relationship with Christ. And thus he is committed to be obedient to God by loving and nurturing the needs of his wife and family, living in a harmonious relationship with each other, being unified in Christ (Gen. 1:27).

The husband, the head of the home, must love his wife just as Christ loves the church, a love that is pure, sincere, constant, and most of all, unconditional. The husband also must be the spiritual leader, physical and emotional provider, and protector of his wife as he nurtures her in the ways of God, not being harsh to her but giving her support, respect, and honor and being gentle as she is the weaker vessel. Husbands must influence his wife spiritually with biblical teaching building her up as he leads and is inspired by God, through which is demonstrated in his action and attitude towards his wife by valuing her as his wife and helpmate.

Husbands must love his wife sacrificially, he caters to her needs spiritually, emotionally, or physically with special care and attention, for she is precious in his eyes. He is thankful, for she is a gift from God. Therefore he desires his wife, rejoices in her happiness, and shares in her pains. He is captivated with her, making her feel loved as the scriptures say, "Husbands that love his wife love himself" (Eph. 5:28).

Husbands ought to love their wives realistically, basing their love on facts and not performance and fancy, and this love includes their faults and failures, that is loving that person because God gave her to him. Husbands should sacrificially, purposefully, willingly, and absolutely love their wives, for submission is mutual between him and his wife, thus blending and giving of themselves to each other. The husbands must be determined that they would sacrifice whatever needed for the sake of the marriage, thus putting nothing as a priority over their wives. By him loving his wife in such a way, he then helps his wife become all that she can be in the family and in Christ. The scriptures say, "Husbands ought to love their wives as their own bodies."

The moment a man and woman gets married, they become one flesh and thus share unity and oneness. Therefore husbands love their wives as if they are loving themselves, and thus he wouldn't hurt himself (Eph. 5:25–28).

Husbands must lead their wife and family with humility and selflessness, having the attitude of Christ in his service towards them, the same love Jesus showed when he washed His disciples' feet, for he was seeking to build them up in the spirit of love for one another in Christ. Therefore the husband's leadership flows from his love for God and his wife, whereby he puts her first, which then is demonstrated in his tenderness and caring affection towards her. They partner up with each other in decision making of the family, for he knows that by him being obedient to God, his family would be blessed and his prayers would not be hindered.

Finally, the husband must remain strong, having the proper understanding of his role as a husband and leader, by being the positive influence for his family and always displaying his love for God and his wife, thereby growing in grace and becoming an inspiration and role model to his children. This exhibition of love from a husband to his wife, loving her as his own self, is apparently what the scriptures admonishes, "For this reason a man leaves his mother and father and is jointed to his wife," being one in a covenant relationship with God (John 13:4–5; Eph. 5:31).

The Bible says, a godly woman is a virtuous woman, she is more precious than rubies, they are wise, compassionate, a blessing to her husband and is faithful in her love towards God and her husband. With that being said, the scriptures commanded for wives to be submissive to their husbands, the purpose of creation and also a curse that was placed on Eve after she ate from the tree of life, because Eve acted independently by rebelling against God and her husband. Wives must be submissive to their husbands out of obedience to God as she honors God and His Word, by placing her trust in God as he gives her His grace and strength to submit. A wife being submissive to her husband allows him to take up the leadership role in their marriage. Hence, in submitting to her husband, she knows she is also submitting and being obedient to God, trusting in His sovereignty, and pleasing God. Wives need not be fearful of being submissive to their husbands if their hope is in God because if the husband is faithful to God's Word, he will use the wives' obedience to accomplish the best for her life (Gen. 3:16).

Submission is a divine purpose of God's lordship and authority. Therefore wives submitting to their husbands is a direct reflection of the submission of the church to Christ. Hence, wives total submission can only come with the help of the Holy Spirit controlling their will and abilities to obey God's command. A wife's submission to her husband is respecting and honoring him, being dignified, devoted, and supportive in order to build him up in the things of God and promoting oneness in the marriage. The wives submission results from her genuine, unconditional love and trust for God and their husbands. Thereby it allows the husband to lead the home more smoothly and effectively as she holds her husband in high esteem, bringing stability, peace, joy, and a positive example to the children on the true embodiment of genuine love. Hence a submissive wife's life is centered around fearing and obeying God, and in the process she becomes wise, generous, and kind. She continues to remain faithful and loving to her family and compassionate to others in need, which exemplifies all the qualities of a virtuous woman that God intended for all women (Col. 3:18).

The concept of wives submitting to their husbands is based on mutual respect and love for God and each other. However, in cases where the husband is being emotionally or physically abusive to their wives, submission is not the option. That kind of behavior clearly differs and is in contrast to God's command of how a husband should love his wife. Therefore the wife must not be submissive to his leadership because the Word of God directly instructs the husband to love and be not harsh to his wife. Also if the husband is leading his wife down a sinful path, thus causing her to sin against God and herself, then she has the right to first secure her own salvation with God rather than to be submissive to her husband.

At the end of life, everyone must give an account for his or her own self before God. Therefore in cases such as these, wives must first secure their own lives and then pray for God's intervention in their husbands' lives. Submission is not living in fear of your husband. Nor is putting his will before God's. Instead it is to affirm and honor in the things of God and his leadership in the home (Col. 3:19).

The Bible teaches parents on how to raise up godly children in the home, and thus God admonishes parents not to provoke their children to anger. Parents must bring up their children the right way in the sight of God. Dealing prudently and wisely with them because they are our responsibility. We deal prudently and wisely with them by showing compassion, love, understanding and directing and encouraging them by teaching them the knowledge and ways of God. It's also the parents responsibility to discipline and set rules, guidelines, and boundaries for children to follow, thereby not allowing them to be rude or disrespectful. Correction is the duty of the parents, as the scriptures admonishes us, "He that spare the rod hates his son but he that love his son correct him." By parents correcting their children in a wise and loving way lets the children be aware of their wrongdoings, thus equipping them to be respectful of themselves and others. This type of correction help them to develop their own self-discipline, and to be obedient to those in authority over them. As a result, it will bring happiness and peace to the family, when parents bring children up in the discipline and instructions of Lord (Prov. 13:24).

Children, obey your parents in the Lord, for this is right. It is a direct command from God. And also children, honor your father and mother, which is the first commandment with a promise, "That thy days maybe long upon the earth." Those two commands shows the great importance God placed on children respecting their parents. Hence, children who honor and obey their parents are also demonstrating their obedience to God, and they will grow up in wisdom as they heed to their parents' instructions, for they will learn the value of respect towards their parents and others.

Those two commands must be adhered to and not be taken lightly, as it was an Old Testament revelation and was also reaffirmed in the

New Testament, the promise of long life when they honor their parents or death of a short-lived life when the command is disobeyed. Therefore, children being obedient to these commands will be blessed of God here on earth as they grow up wisely and eventually develop the habits of respect for those in authority as they go through life (Ex. 20:12; Deut. 5:15; Eph. 6:1–2).

Children who choose not to honor and obey their parents will bring great trouble into their lives for disobedience is one of the tricks of Satan, for all he wants is to destroy as many souls as possible. Jesus specifically tells us these words to show the importance of obeying and honoring parents, "He that curse father or mother let him die the death." This is a curse of death that is placed on children who chooses to not to honor and obey their parents and disobey God's instructions. Children ought to take heed, be obedient to parents, and grow into adulthood showing respect to others so they can live a happier and fulfilled life because obeying their parents in everything is pleasing to God. The Bible admonishes, "Children must hear their father's instructions and forsake not their mother's teaching, tie them around your neck. When you walk they will lead you, and when you lie down, they will watch over you and when you awake, they will talk with you." Therefore, children must take the instructions received from both parents and adopt them into their adult life, for these commandments are a lamp and the teaching of light for them (Prov. 6:20–23; Col. 3:20).

Jesus' obedience was shown to His heavenly Father and His earthly parents when he was in the temple, teaching being obedient to His call to His heavenly Father. However, when he went back to Nazareth with His earthly parents, not only did he obey, he also submitted to their authority over Him. Jesus' obedience is a perfect example that children of today's time ought to learn. A child who values his or her parents words in both his or her's attitudes and actions will give them the favor of God in their lives. The Bible tells us that a wise son takes heed to his father's instruction.

Children obeying and honoring parents, shows love for God and their parents, for it is the right thing to do. In essence, it helps them develop a godly lifestyle and a relationship in the present and future as they keep God's laws and commandments in their hearts as long life, and peace are added to them. Obeying parents is children's duty and obligation towards their parents, thereby creating an everlasting relationship that is unified in love (Prov. 3:1–2).

Sarah demonstrates how a submissive wife ought to be, when God came to Abraham and told him to move from his country. Without asking any questions, Sarah obeyed her husband and moved on faith according to the instructions of God. Sarah's desire was for God and her husband, by her submitting to Abraham, she had faith that God would do what was best for their lives. Thus she followed her husband's leading. Sarah took up her role as her husband's helpmate, also as a submissive wife so the plans of God could be fulfilled in Abraham's life. Sarah demonstrated her submissiveness by calling her husband "Lord," which showed her love and respect towards her husband, for she held him in high esteem. By honoring her husband, she expressed her faith in God. God blessed Sarah because of her faith and for being a submissive wife, whereby she received the power to conceive and strength to bring forth a baby even at her old age, thus fulfilling the promise of God to Abraham. Sarah was commended in the Bible as a submissive wife and a woman of faith, but mostly as the mother of many nations, for she was precious and blessed of God (Gen. 17:15–16).

The life of Abraham and Sarah should be a great model and a source encouragement to us on the principles of how a godly home should be. A home built strong in faith, obedience, love, self-sacrificing, and submissiveness. To building a godly home that God blesses, it must be built on genuine love for God and each other, respect, and mutual understanding, which is based on godly values and biblical truths, the starting points of establishing a godly home. It regards no one superior than the other, for we all are subjected unto God. living in unity, respect and showing love in everything, allowing our faith and love in God as our motivation. Therefore, keeping prayer a frequent element and instilling these principles in the home, by exercising forbearance honestly with each other and respect, there will be togetherness, love, and happiness in the home (Phil. 1:4).

Let love, faith reign and grow throughout when building a godly home.

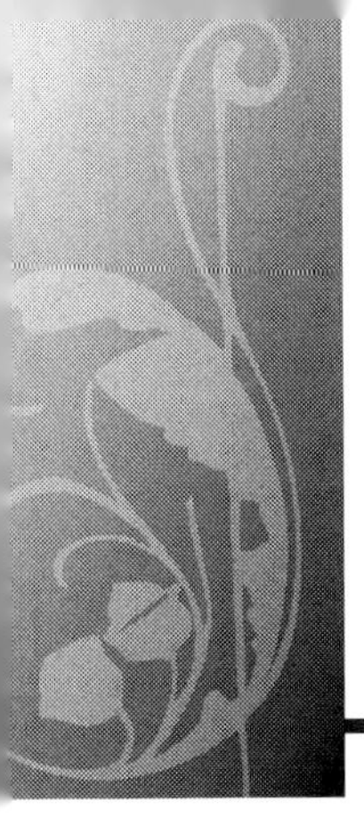

Anticipating Jesus' Return

In accordance to the book of Daniel, Revelation, and the Old Testament prophets, of all the prophecies that was prophesied regarding the coming Messiah, all have already been fulfilled. However, the Bible tells us about prophecies of an ultimate future, the second coming of Christ, which is yet to be fulfilled. In the Word of God, it tells of two culminating events that will involve the return of Jesus Christ: the rapture and the second coming of Jesus Christ to earth.

These two events are separate. The Rapture is when Jesus Christ will take His church as "His bride." Those who believed and trusted in Him as their Lord and Savior will be taken back to heaven with Him, leaving only those who rejected Him on the earth. God will give a period of seven years to the earth after the Rapture.

At the end of this time period, the second coming of Jesus Christ will take place. However, although these two events are a bit similar, they are totally different, for in the Rapture, all the believers of Christ will be taken out of this world. And in the second coming, Jesus will execute judgment against this evil world and thus place an end to its existence (Matt. 24:38).

Both the Rapture and the second coming of Christ will take place at different locations. During the Rapture of the church, Jesus Christ will descend in clouds above the earth as he ushers in the church, for he will not directly be on earth. He will be in the clouds, and this is known to believers, for it is the blessed hope in Christ. Therefore we, His followers, live uprightly and godly lives while we wait for the appearance of the glory of our Lord and Savior, because Jesus Christ is our hope. His imminent return could happen at anytime. Thus we live in the power of the indwelling Holy Spirit, a life of purity honoring Christ.

At the second coming of Christ, the scriptures tells us that Jesus Christ's feet will be on Mount of Olives in Jerusalem here on earth, the same place from whence he left and ascended back to heaven. God cannot lie, and His Word is true. It's very clear and a strong indication that both the Rapture and His second coming is eminent, which is a source of comfort to us His followers, knowing we will spend eternity with Jesus Christ and escape judgment.

The Bible says that Jesus will return in power and great glory and will be judging the earth by pouring out His wrath on the nations and all those who rejected Him, a reminder to all of His hatred towards sin (Titus 2:12–13; Zech. 14:4).

The Rapture is the end of the church age, the assurance of God's blessing for His followers here on earth and our final journey to our eternal home with Christ as he showers us with His favor and love by taking us out of this ungodly world.

The scriptures tell us that no one knows when the Rapture will take place. Jesus Himself spoke about this event, "On that day and hour no man knows not the angels but only His father knows." Therefore, the Rapture could take place at anytime without warning. Thus, we must be watchful. The Rapture is the separation of the believers in Christ out of this sinful world, which will come as a surprise to those who are unsaved. During the Rapture of the church, there will not be any judgment of the saints. Instead, we will be rewarded in heaven for our works. The Rapture is known as the first resurrection, the resurrection of the life and the church, both the dead and alive in Christ, this is necessary in order for the tribulation period to begin so the Antichrist can be revealed, this is the beginning of the tribulation in this present world (Matt. 24:36–42; Rev. 20:6).

The Rapture of the church is a happy expectation, a comforting hope, and a glorious majestic procession of the saints of Christ, those who are in Christ in this present world. We are taken out of this world before the judgment proceeding His second coming, and we will be protected from God's wrath. Jesus Himself left with us this reassurance and a comforting promise, "I go and prepare a place for you, I will come again, and receive you unto myself; that where I am, there ye may be also," the hope of all believers in Christ that he will come back for His faithful followers. All the saints of Christ will meet Him in the clouds, starting from the Old Testament saints, they will be raised first, followed by the present-day saints, then those who are alive in Christ. Our bodies will be changed from mortal to immortal glorified bodies where we will be like Christ. Therefore, we all must be prayerful and watchful, anxiously awaiting His return and not to be like the days of Noah. The Rapture is an instantaneous hidden event that can happen at any time (John 14:3; 1 Thess. 4:17).

Immediately after the Rapture of the church, seven years of tribulation follow. And it's when God finalizes His judgment on the unbelieving world, the tribulation is divided into two halves. The first three and half years are known as the tribulation period. In this time period the world will be spinning out of control, morally declining, religious apostasy is in full effect, and the world is falling away from the true doctrine of Christ and embracing the false religion cult. At this point the Antichrist will make his move.

For the nations of this world will be seeking peace amongst each other, the unknown Antichrist, someone with great power, would negotiate seven years of peace between Israel and its enemies, acting as the great protector and friend of Israel.

In the beginning of the seven years of the tribulation, the Antichrist will make a covenant of peace treaty with the nations of this world promising peace, during which everything will be relatively peaceful. Things would seem to be going well, for there will be peace, marriages and births. However, evil will still be dominant, and life will continue as normal because they are experiencing the peace they were seeking. Unbeknownst to these ungodly people they didn't know this peace will only last for a short period of time (Dan. 9:27).

In this first half of the tribulation, there will be a rise of false prophets, which will result in tremendous sin, iniquity, immorality, and rebellion against God. Everything God said was wrong becomes right, and true love will be hard to find in the hearts of man. In this period of the tribulation, the wrath of God will greatly intensify in this world, for the world will be godless without the gospel of Christ, hence, Jesus Himself tells us what will take place in the tribulation period, "It will be the beginning of sorrow," for sin will proceed rapidly without hindrance for there would be terrible wickedness on the earth.

However, even in this tribulation period, God shows His redemptive mercy and grace by sending two witnesses from heaven whom the Holy Spirit empowers to preach the true Word of God to the people of the world. These two great witnesses of Christ were given great power, and thus the scriptures tells us, "They had power to shut heaven so no rain can fall also power over the water bodies on earth." And as such, they go throughout the earth, preaching the Word of God and performing miraculous signs in the presence of the people (Rev. 11–12; Matt. 24:8).

The Bible tells us that many people, both Jews and Gentiles, believe and trust in Jesus Christ as their Savior, thereby giving glory unto God in the tribulation period. And as a result of their turning to Christ, the Antichrist persecutes most of them for their belief in Christ.

In the second half of the seven-year peace treaty, the Antichrist will break his covenant with the nations, revealing his true identity, and take complete power of the world, which then will clearly indicate that the ending of age is very close and the returning of Christ to earth will be soon. This period, the abomination of desolation is referred to in the Bible as the "great tribulation."

After the two witnesses of God have finished their testimony of Christ, the Antichrist, "the beast," will fight and kill them because they have brought the testimonies of Jesus Christ. However, after three and a half days, the two witnesses will come back to life and taken back to heaven. The Antichrist will then set an image of himself in the temple of God and declares himself as God, whom the people must worship by having his mark written on their forehead or on their hands (Rev. 13:17).

In the great tribulation, there will be great persecution, agony, and distress, as Satan, who will be finally cast out of heaven completely; the Antichrist; and his followers will war against those remnants of Israel who believed in Christ. However, God supernaturally protects His faithful seed, Israel, and in this war, the Antichrist is killed, and Satan brings him back to life, which he will use as a ploy to deceive more people in taking his mark and worshiping him. The Antichrist will then blasphemy against God, His name, His tabernacle, and those who dwell in heaven, as more power has been given unto him.

Satan, the Antichrist, and the false prophet created a religion, they made a decree that all mankind must worship the Antichrist as they perform great signs and wonders, thus deceiving and putting great pressure on the people into getting the mark of the beast so they can buy or sell goods.

Despite all the pressure placed by the Satanic Trinity, 144,000 true followers of Christ refuse to take the mark of the beast and die for the cause of Christ. For this, they are called blessed according the Word of God (Rev. 13:1–8, 14:13).

The nations wanted to be free from under the control of the Antichrist and decided to fight against the Satanic Trinity, while in the process to war, the scriptures tells us, "The heavens opened and behold a white horse, and he that sat on Him was called Faithful and True and in righteousness he doth judge and make war," and on Him is written the name "KING OF KINGS AND LORD OF LORDS."

This is known as the great day of the Lord. It is the second coming of Jesus Christ, which is the fulfillment of all prophecies on the second coming of Christ to reclaim this world from the hands of Satan and to establish truth and justice on the earth. The Bible tells us that out of Jesus' mouth comes a sharp sword, "which is the Word of God," and he destroys the wicked people throughout all the earth with just His Word, and their bodies became food for the fowls of the air. The Antichrist, the false prophet, and those who worshiped him were cast alive into the lake of fire burning with brimstone. Satan was bound with great chains and cast into the bottomless pit, where he will remain for a thousand years, after which he will be released for a little season (Rev. 11, 12, 19:1–21).

After Jesus regains the world from Satan, he will reign a thousand years in Jerusalem with the faithful saints of the tribulation period, both those alive and martyred here on earth to fulfill His promise to Abraham and his believing descendant, where they would have the promised land for eternity. Jesus would rule over them as their Messiah. This is Jesus rewarding the faithful saints as he ministers and rules over them so they could experience peace, safety, and righteousness throughout the earth, for nature will be restored to its original form with all its beauty and splendor as they bask in the glory of God.

In the millennium, all mankind will worship Jesus Christ and continue in the faith, thereby obeying Him in all things he has set out before them as the glory of God and His righteousness will fill the world. In the millennium years, mankind's life span will be longer, there will be marriages, deaths, and new births during this time because life would be as normal with the exception that it is now under the reign of Jesus Christ. There will be peace, comfort, and happiness for the tribulation saints to enjoy life (Gen. 12).

Before the millennium comes to an end, Jesus will releases Satan from the bottomless pit for a short period for him to go throughout the nation to deceive people. Many of the people will rebelled against Christ and joined forces with Satan against Christ. The scriptures tells us that they are like the sands of the sea, that rebelled against Christ and His Lordship and warring against Him in the battle known as Gog and Magog.

This event marks the last rebellion against Christ, for during this rebellion war, God sends down fire from heaven, which devours Satan and his followers. And they all were cast into the lake of fire and brimstone to join the Antichrist and the false prophet. In the closure of the millennium years, Jesus will perform the resurrection of those who died in Christ during the millennium years and those names that were in the Book of Life. Then the Bible tells us, "The sea and earth gave up the unsaved dead." And those whose names are not found in the Book of Life, Jesus Christ will judge them according to their works, and they would be cast into the lake of fire and everlasting punishment, which is the second death (Rev. 20:1–15).

Jesus made a promise to His disciples, "I go to prepare a place for you; I will come again, and receive you unto myself, that where I am there you will be also," which is the blessed hope of all His followers, the glorious and eternal reunion with Christ. The old earth and the heavens will be destroyed and found no more for there is no place for them, the scriptures tells us, "A new heaven, earth and Jerusalem came down from heaven," where Christ will live with His saints in holy perfection and righteousness.

It is important for us to know that the new earth and Jerusalem is being prepared and built in heaven. It has twelve gates that inscribes the twelve tribes of Israel because God chose Israel to be a light to the nations. The gates will never be shut, for there wouldn't be any night. In this new heaven, earth, and Jerusalem, we will reign with Christ forever in our glorified bodies, free from sin, evil, sickness, suffering, and death, for God shall wipe away all the tears from our eyes. The scripture tells us "God is the Alpha and Omega and the beginning and the end". He will continually be with us (Rev. 21:1; Is. 65:17, 66:22, John 14:3).

In the New Jerusalem, there will be no need for a temple because the presence and the glory of God shines as the light, which permeates and illuminates the entire heaven and earth. Hence, there would be no the sun and the moon. The new heaven and the new earth will not be separated because the presence of God will be with us always. Thus Jesus said, "I will give unto him that thirst of the fountain of the water of life freely," for we shall inherit all things that is of God.

Jesus also tells us, "Blessed are the pure in heart for they shall see God." And as followers of Christ, we will live, reign and see Him face-to-face, living in the abundance of His blessings and provisions that flows from the throne of God. Living life eternal with Christ in pure joy, happiness, and worship, for we will be glorifying God (Matt. 5:8).

We the followers of Christ cannot grow careless and become worldly minded, believing Jesus Christ will not return. Instead, we ought to be vigilant and watchful, knowing we are living in the last days and can see the signs of His coming. In anticipation of His coming, we must draw closer to holiness, directing our hearts towards Christ preparing our mind, body, and soul, remaining watchful, eagerly awaiting His return. Putting on the spirit of grace and sanctification. Being spiritually minded and having a high level of awareness. Rejecting sin, wise to things that are taking place in the world and securing our souls from eternal damnation. Living godly and holy lives by letting our light of witness and righteousness shine in this dark world of sin while spreading the gospel with urgency. Making it our primary priority to share the gospel with others and warn them of the imminent return of Jesus Christ and Him putting an end to sin.

Speaking also of His punishment and judgment towards all who rejected Him. Encouraging them to follow Christ so they too can enjoy the glorious, joyful event of His second coming and experience eternal life with Him (1 Thess. 1:10).

We consume ourselves in prayer and supplication to God and pursue the things that involves the kingdom of God, having an honest, faithful understanding of His teachings. Remaining committed to the faith, being steadfast and settled in the hope of the gospel. Living every day with confidence, identifying ourselves with Christ in His death and resurrection under grace. Full in readiness and faithfulness, knowing that one day we will be worthy enough to stand before Him and receive our crowns. Having an exciting vision of His return helps us overcome our problems, it provides us with joy and happiness deep down inside, knowing that we will be reunited with Jesus. Exercising patience to His coming, we remain awakened out of our slumber, having our lamps trim, awaiting the coming of the King of Kings and Lord of Lords (1 John 3:3).

Judgment Day of Christ is fast approaching;
choose Christ and eternal life.

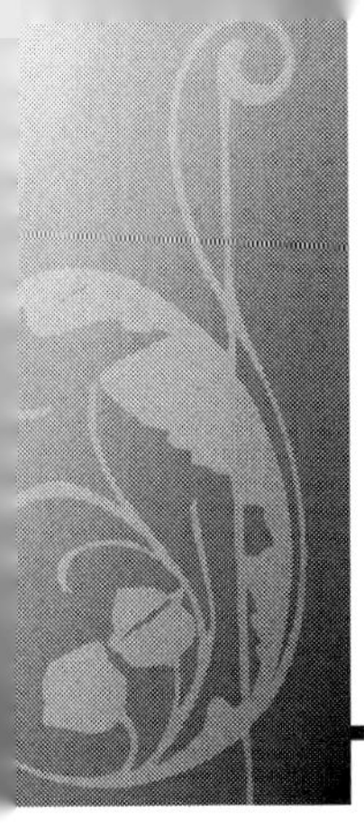

The Supremacy and Sovereignty of God

The sovereignty of God is His supremacy, holiness, and righteousness, he is the Most High God of Heaven. Nothing can hinder His ultimate power, and there is none like Him. God dominion rule is eternal. His divine sovereignty implies that he is infinite and is eternal. He sits on the throne in heaven and rules the entire universe, for he existed before the world was formed. He is the source of all creation and has all rights over it. Everything in the universe solely depends on God for survival because they are all under His divine will and purpose. The universe and all the heavens under the sun tells how great and marvelous the sovereignty of God really is, for they are all under His subjection and is control by Him. Nothing happens without His approval and permission, for he is supreme in power and authority. God's sovereignty extends to all things of His creation, and therefore he is not limited to time or space, he governs all creation with righteousness, maintaining continuous stability of creation, His power is everywhere, enlightening things seen and unseen in the world (Gen. 1:1; Is. 46:9–10).

There is no other power in the heavens nor on the earth that is greater than God's, as they were all created by Him and for Him, he holds and binds them together, which symbolizes His sovereignty and His greatness. God's sovereignty is characterized in His character and authority. He is active in everything that happens in creation, thereby having the power to do whatever he desires, and as the scriptures tells us, "He does as he pleases with the powers of heaven, the people of the earth and no one can hold back His hands."

His supremacy and power are demonstrated in His Word, with

Moses and the children of Israel in there existing from Egypt with the division of the Red Sea, and when he ordered the sun to stand still. God's name speaks of His sovereignty as seen in the Old Testament. "Yahweh," which is Almighty God, and subsequently God told Moses to tell the people of Israel "I Am That I Am." sent him to lead them out of Egypt so they would know that the only true God was present and active. His sovereignty is revealed in His Word and in every circumstance in our pathway, whether it be a current or present situation in this world. He is the same God yesterday, today, and forevermore, and he is always in control (Ex. 3:14, 6:3).

God's sovereignty is found in His deity. It is who he is, the ruler of His eternal plans for creation, which is characterized in all His attributes, love, mercy, and grace for he is the beginning and the end. He knows the past, present, and future. There is no limit to His vast knowledge. It is beyond human comprehension. God knows exactly what needs to be done and at what time, for all wisdom and knowledge is given unto Him. Salvation is God's sovereign work, whereby he chooses whom he will save, which is a gift. This process was predestined even before the foundation of the earth, whereby he calls us according to His purpose and plans, hence forming us into an image of His Son Jesus Christ. God is not subjected to the decisions of others; hence, the purposes of His choosing is hidden in His secret council of His own. As he said in His Word, "My thoughts are not your thoughts, neither are you ways my ways, and as the heavens are higher than the earth so are my ways higher than your ways and my thoughts than your thoughts." Therefore, there is nothing anyone can do but accept God's sovereignty, and our responsibility to the gospel of Christ (Is. 46:9, 55:8–9).

God is all powerful, for all power is given unto Him both in heaven and earth, no one can hold Him back because he sits on the throne in heaven, directing all things and conforming them to His will. Therefore we ought to fear, honor, and serve God. His sovereignty gives Him the freedom to do as he pleases with His blessings, compassion, humanity, and loving kindness to those who fear and love Him as he bestows His righteousness to those in obedience to His command, thus giving them confidence in knowing that His power is all powerful. The power of God is omnipotent. It is unlimited and immeasurable to creation and nature, he has the ability to change time and season. He removes kings and sets up kings, which demonstrates His supremacy and dominance over everything in this universe. His powers are manifested in Him for nothing is impossible with Him, even the winds and the rains obey His command just as he spoke them in this world, "Let there be," speaking things into existence as if it were, thus demonstrating the greatness of His powers (Gen. 1:3).

His omnipresence demonstrated also His authority over mankind, for he is everywhere at the same time. He is not restricted to time or space because he has no spatial limitation, he is bigger than space and is present in all space. His presence continues from the beginning of creation and even unto eternity, for he is sovereign. Nothing can be hidden from Him, the scriptures tells us, "The eyes of the Lord is everywhere beholding evil and good." God's omnipresence is through His Holy Spirit and felt in the heart of all those who receive His salvation, which is the appropriation of His mercy and grace through the blood of Jesus. We cannot never go beyond His presence because he is always with us, guiding, straightening, and protecting. God is also omniscient. All knowing, he encompasses the past, present, and future of this universe. There is no limit to His vast knowledge and understanding, for he knows us while in the womb and he knows us better than we even know ourselves. The scriptures tells us that God knows the numbers of every hair on our head and that His eyes are in every place, beholding evil and good, searching the hearts of mankind, for he understands all the desires and thoughts of mankind (Ps. 139:7–14; 1 Chr. 28:9).

Jesus Christ, the Son of God, also has the same supremacy and sovereignty as God the Father, it is in His God nature that affirms Him as His Son. Jesus Christ has the ultimate power, authority, and glory of God. He is the firstborn of every created being. He is the Son of God and the heir and ruler of everything in this universe. In having all the fullness of God dwelling in Him, the scriptures tells us, "In the beginning was the Word and the Word was with God and the Word was God."

Jesus Christ was the Word, which was in the beginning with God. Jesus Christ pre-existed with God, and he is the representation of God the Father, having the radiance of His glory, which is found in His deity, for he is also God, as the scripture enlightens us. Jesus Christ is sovereign by virtue of His genetics, he is the only begotten Son of the true and living God.

Therefore as His Son, all power and authority in both heaven and on earth was given unto Him by God, the ultimate ruler of everything. And with His power, Jesus sustains this whole universe with the power of His is word, thus holding them in His hands (Col. 1:18, 2:9).

Jesus' supremacy and sovereignty was demonstrated in His birth, whereby he was conceived by the Holy Spirit and born of a woman in the flesh with both the God and human nature. He is the Son incarnate, for he is the invisible image of God, His Father, and in Him is all the deity of God, thus making Him God and man at the same time, "the God-man."

As a testimony to Jesus' supremacy and sovereignty after His baptism, God the Father spoke from heaven saying, "This is my Beloved Son in whom am well pleased," thereby acknowledging Jesus Christ as His Son as he lived on earth in both the nature of God and man. Jesus having those two natures, would play a vital role in providing salvation to mankind as he sacrificed His life on the cross for our sins, thus giving us access to God through His blood, which was shed on Calvary and His resurrection from the dead on the third day.

Jesus Christ is God incarnate, for he has omnipotent power, which was seen in all the miracles he performed in His earthly ministry, such as raising Lazarus from the dead, healing the sick, feeding the multitudes etc, these signifies and cements His supremacy. In essence, His exhibition of power shows that he holds the power of life and death in His hands and that same power will be demonstrated again and seen by all in His second coming to earth as he puts an end to this evil world (Is. 9:6; John 5:25–29).

Jesus has supremacy and sovereignty powered over death, for he is the firstborn of the dead. He was first to raise from the dead with a spiritual and immortal body. Thus he demonstrated His preeminence in all things, for he is the full and complete godhead with the fullness of God dwelling in Him. Jesus Christ, who knew no sin, sacrificed His life by dying for the sins of the world; His resurrection set Him apart from others, for he has risen and is alive today, sitting at the right hand of God the Father as the high priest, making intercession for the saints, the mediator between God and mankind. His death and resurrection give us a new covenant that is filled with His grace and lovc, hence putting an end to the old covenant, which was filled with laws.

Thereby granting to us an easier way to be saved through salvation, where we can receive God's forgiveness of our sins, saving us from eternal damnation. Jesus' death and resurrection, created a new creation, the church (the body), whereas he is the supreme head, ruler, and founder. Without the head (Christ Jesus), the body cannot function because His resurrection is the basis of our faith, which leads to salvation (Col. 1:18).

Jesus Christ is the Savior of the world, the spotless Lamb of God, and head of the church. He died for mankind, and as head, he continues to direct the works of the church through the presence of the Holy Spirit, which indwells and empowers us to continue in His earthly mission that he started while on earth. As head of the church, Jesus nourishes it spiritually through His Word so the body can hold fast to Him as Lord, thereby we express His nature and character throughout the church in a visible way, and bringing glorification to Him. As representative of Christ, we the church must live holy and blameless lives in His sight and be the light, which shines brightly in this world, hence demonstrating to the world that Jesus Christ is Lord and Savior, and in Him can be found grace, salvation, and righteousness (Eph. 1:22–23).

Jesus Himself said, "I and my father are one." This signifies that Jesus Christ has equal authority with God the father, and all His Words are true, complete, and final. As followers of Christ we must acknowledge and believe that Jesus as the divine Son of God, who holds the same power of God and was sent by God. Jesus also made mention of Abraham when he said, "Before Abraham was, I am," which also signifies that Jesus is superior over Abraham. It was also noted from the story of Sodom and Gomarrah, where Abraham met Jesus along with the two angels who came to destroy Sodom, and also again when Lord came and told him his wife would conceive. Abraham addressed God as "my Lord."

In contrast, the superiority of Jesus, we know that Jesus Christ is the Son of God, who had supernatural greatness and powers and came to be the divine object of faith, and our Savior, whom the whole kingdoms of this world will revere and worship, for he was once dead and rose on the third day and is alive today.

On the other hand, Abraham was known as a friend of God, a great man of faith, a great leader, and the father of many nations. However, Abraham is dead and no longer alive. Thus, God used Abraham to be a great example of faith and what it takes to be a righteous man and a spiritual leader to the world (Gen. 18–19).

Jesus Christ is sovereign and superior over Moses, the prophets, and the Old Testament high priest. Moses was a faithful servant of the house of God who led the people of Israel out of Egypt and toward God. He was also the mediator between God and the people of Israel. He only had limited access to God. He foretold of Jesus' coming, and God gave him the Old Testament laws. Moses was an apostle sent by God, and Aaron, his brother, was the first high priest of the Old Testament who represented the people before God. He was also the spokesperson for Moses before Pharaoh.

In contrast, Jesus was the faithful Son of God and the builder of the house, which is the Word of God. He have all access to God, His Father, the mediator for all mankind who intercedes on our behalf to God. God sent Jesus to earth to free mankind from the bondage of sin, thus putting an end to the laws that was given to Moses. Jesus Christ is the supreme high priest who knows no sin and represents us before God, His death was the perfect sacrifice that removed the wrath of God from us. And now we have direct access to God through Jesus Christ, who is both the High Priest after the order of Melchisedec, King of Kings, and the master of the house, His church, and His people (Heb. 3:1–6; Deut. 18:15).

Jesus is superior to all creations, both visible and invisible, which includes Satan and every other spiritual power in the universe. Satan was thrown out of heaven because he wanted to be like God. He is now ruler of this world. However, Jesus Christ is over all Satan's diabolical rules by His divine powers and righteousness, and one day Christ will take back the world from under the ruler and influences of Satan.

Satan, as we noted from the story of Job, cannot do anything to mankind without the permission of God. He is limited to what he can do, for he is still under the control of God. Thus he could not kill Job. However, Satan has the power of death but it must be permitted by God. Secondly, Jesus told Simon Peter that Satan wants to sift/test him. Thus Jesus prayed for Peter so this faith failed not. This shows us again that Satan must seek permission from God before he does anything to anyone.

Finally Jesus, superiority above Satan is demonstrated when Satan tempted Him in the wilderness. God the father gave Satan permission to tempt Jesus, as clearly stated, "Jesus was led by the holy spirit in the wilderness." In each temptation, Jesus showed His authority of the Word of God. God is ruler over Satan, whom God created as an angel. However, due to his pride, he wanted to be God, which got him cast out of heaven. Thus he set up his kingdom on earth, deceiving mankind (Job 1:12, 2:1–6; Heb. 2:14; Matt. 4:1).

It is important to know that God is sovereign, and when he created this world, everything he created was good. He did not create sin, sin entered the world as an act of rebellion again God. He created mankind in His own image with a free will. Therefore, we were made free, having the ability to make our own choices. Adam chose to be disobedient by his rebellion, which bring him spiritual death. Thus sin entered the world. Sin originated with Lucifer/Satan, he was rebellious against God and thrown out of heaven. Sin is a rebellious attitude or action against the laws of God, it is lawlessness and a violation of God holy law. Mankind has the freedom to obey God, which leads them to righteous living or they can follow their own inclinations by disobeying God, which will lead them away from God and into eternal damnation. Through Adam, sin entered the world and was passed down through all his generations, his descendants also inherited the sin virus from him, bringing spiritual death to all mankind, as we are all born with the impulse towards sin and evil.

Although mankind sins against God, he was still merciful toward us that he provided a way to escape spiritual death. God does not delight in punishment. Thus he made a way so we can come to repentance through His Son Jesus Christ and experience eternal life (Gen. 1:31, 2:16–17; Rom. 5:12).

King Nebuchadnezzar, a pagan king and a great military and political power for he ruled the nation of Babylon, dominating all the world's powers. However, with all his power, it could not compared to the power of God. God demonstrated His supremacy to King Nebuchadnezzar on three different occasions; first when Daniel interpreted his dream. Thus he said to Daniel, "Your God is a God of gods and Lord of kings and a revealer of secrets." Second, in the fiery furnace, King Nebuchadnezzar said, "I saw the four men walking in midst of the fire and the form of the fourth is the Son of God." And finally, Daniel again interpreted his second dream, after which King Nebuchadnezzar became like a beast of the field for seven seasons.

At the end of those seasons, King Nebuchadnezzar said, "I lifted up my eyes unto heaven, and mine understanding returned unto me; and I blessed the most High God, praise and worship Him that live forever, whose dominion is an everlasting dominion and His kingdom is from generation to generation." It's only when King Nebuchadnezzar submitted and humbled himself before God, did he truly accept and recognize the supremacy and sovereignty of the God of heaven (Dan. 2–4).

All mankind must acknowledge the sovereignty and supremacy of God by being humble and submissive to His will, thereby relying solely upon His divine power and authority. The more we accept His sovereignty in this world and our lives, it would then prompt us to obedience to Him. God's sovereignty is geared to the glorification and exaltation of Him in our worship and praise, being confident that we are serving the true and living God. Everything is under His control and are subjected to Him, as God said, "The heaven is my throne, and the earth is my footstool." Therefore we His followers, having full knowledge of His sovereignty, should never lose our perspective of God's majestic power and His greatness. We place our focus completely upon Him as the Supreme Ruler over the affairs of the entire world. Trusting only His promises and creating strong relationship with Him, a place of pure comfort and rest that prompts us to worship and praise Him in spirit and truth. God created this universe. God sustains the world. They are all for the glory of God. We exist because God created us by His sovereign choice, and right now he is sustaining us for His glory (Is. 66:1; Ps. 48:1).

Jesus Christ is the ultimate rule, authority, and power over all creation.

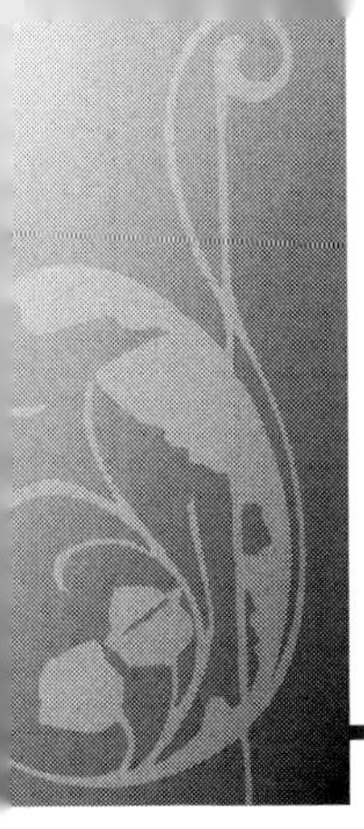

My Testimony, My Life

Imagine growing up in a country where everyone looks at you negatively, and even in this present time as an adult, being looked down on just because of who your father is. Well, that is my life story, the only child of my father. First, I must say that I loved my father with all my heart, for he was my father and the only person who truly loved me, back then, all we had was each other to lean and depend on.

Sadly my father died in 2011, and I'm so grateful he had someone in his life who truly loved and appreciated him. May his soul rest in eternal peace. My father was a troubled man due to something that accidentally transpired in his life at the age of twelve, and as a result of that incident, he never knew no peace in his life which turned him into an alcoholic. My father was a nice, caring man who once you get to know him you would love him, however the people of my country did not give him a chance, thus they looked down on him and regarded him as a nobody. And as his only child, that unrest and treatment triggered down to me. However, I embraced who my father was, and live a life that would make my father proud, the village people were shocked for they could not believe that I was his child. With such cloud hovering over my life as his child made me much stronger so that I could be the person of comfort and love for him while he was alive, and he was so proud of me. My father knew I had his back and would love him no matter what, for we were alone in this world together with no peace of mind due to the stigma that others in our country placed on us.

My father is gone now, and oh, how I wish he was alive today, he was the one I could talk to when am down, he listened while I vented my problems, he encourage and give me advise always being the voice of reasoning. I miss him so much for he and my children are all I have in this world. I often ask myself why did God take him away from me he was all I had. Anyway God knows why he took him from me.

I realized from a young age that God had His hands on my life, even as a little child growing up. Oh, my life was so hard back then and even now, but through it all, God has kept me, and I'm grateful. This is my story.

As the only child of my father, at three months, my father took me from my mother and gave me to his mother to raise. And thus my story began. I can remember things that transpired in my life from the early age of four, and those memories were not pleasant. My father was known as one the baddest man in our community. He was also an alcoholic, as drinking was what he did to forget his past, but yet the people gave him no peace of mind. They would pick fights and argue with him when he was drunk so they might have a chance overpower him. Yet even when drunk, they could not overpower him. When he was sober, he did not talk much, as he was a serious person and knew how the people felt about him, thus they did not trouble him because he was a physically strong man.

My father's mother was old in age. She suffered two previous strokes, and she also had elephantiasis in one of her foot, which hampered her walking abilities. Thus she had to walk with a walking stick and me to help here walk.

When my grandmother goes to the village center, I would lead her by holding her hand over the bushy and rocky road. However in leading her, when I was not walking fast enough, she would take her walking stick and hit me on my head, bursting open my head with her walking stick. I was between five and six years at that time. Today I still have the scar marks all over my head from those hits to my head, and as a result, I began suffering from severe migraine headaches. I don't think my father ever knew anything about this because it would have been disastrous for my grandmother. Therefore it was for the best that he did not know.

Being placed in such a terrible position in life, I had learn and develop survival skills. Even at such a young age, I would have to find means and ways to feed myself. I can remember digging up sweet potatoes out of the ground and eating them raw, along going to other family house to get food. I was left basically to myself, for I was my own boss. I went to and left school when I wanted, as the teachers and the people of the community were afraid to say or do anything to me because of the fear of my father.

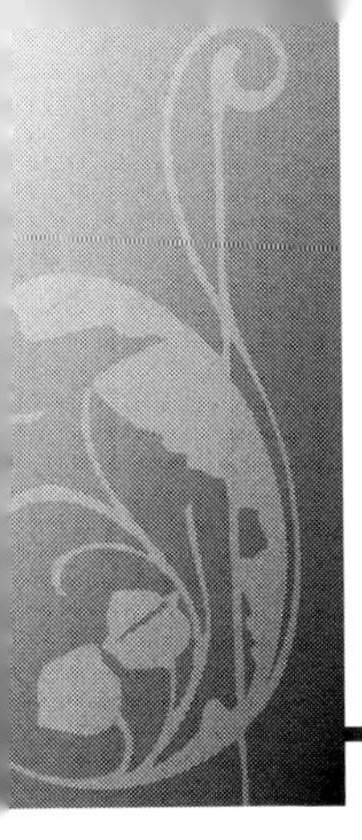

I Encountered a Stranger

There's a saying that say God's timing is the best and he always shows up right on time. Such was the case for me, God showed up just in time for me to preserve and save my life. At the age of six, one day, my grandmother sent me to the center corner shop to buy something for her. I really don't remember what it was. As I was in the shop, the high school bus came and dropped off children for my village, the driver would give the children from the next village time to go into the shop to get candies, gum, and so on.

Now on that day, one of the high school girls from the next village saw me in the shop, came to me and said to me, "You look like us." She asked me what my name and who my was father. So I told her. I never saw her before in my life. She didn't get back on the school bus. Instead she asked me to take her to where I lived.

I took her home, she then told my grandmother that I was her niece and my mother was her sister. I never knew I had any other family but my father's family, for no one ever came to look for me, although they knew about my existence, not to mention that our villages were just a fifteen-minute drive away.

My aunt told my grandmother all about my mother and her family and said I had an older sister as well. And that was how I knew I had a mother and other family. After that day, my aunt would visit me on the weekends. And sometimes after school, she'd bring food and clothes for me so I could get accustomed to her.

After months of visiting me, she asked my grandmother if she could take me to her home to meet my other family, which my grandmother agreed. I was not a normal child at all to be honest at that time, I had the behavior of a wild child, I was afraid of people due to the fact that I was a lone child with basically no parenting, and people would shun me just because of my father.

My aunt took me to meet my newly found family from my mothers side, I was afraid of them. I cried a lot and followed my auntie everywhere because they were strangers to me. In my newly found family, I met my other grandmother, grandfather, older sister, and uncles, and from then onward, my aunt would take me every weekend to spend time with them so I could get accustomed and form a relationship with the family.

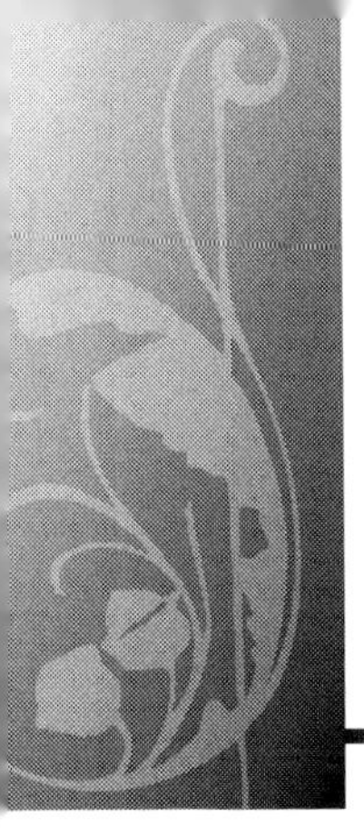

God's Merciful Hands on My Life

After my weekly weekend visits with my newly found family, my aunt asked my father's mother if she would give me to her so I could live with my new family because my grandmother was old and my father was about to go back to jail again. So my grandmother agreed and gave me to her. It's amazing how God does work. My grandmother gave me up that weekend, and before the next week was finished, my grandmother died and was buried within the span of days after giving me over to my auntie.

With that being said, we can see that God's timing is always the best, and he works all things according to His plan and purpose for my life, it was not a coincidence or sheer luck that I was in that shop that day. God purposed it to be that way so he could made a way out for me to survive and live.

One year after living with my new family, I met other members who came from abroad, however one particular person was not as welcoming to me at all, which made the reunion not a happy one. Instead it was a very terrible, sad and painful experience, such emotional pain a seven-year-old all excited should never experience, anyway all I can say is that God is good.

My grandmother and grandfather were there for me, especially when my father would come by drunk. They stayed with me whenever he visited me because by living with this family I knew normalcy I became terrified and afraid of my father. Yet I knew he loved and needed me.

As I grew in age, experiencing all the pressure of being my father's child, I continue to keep my head high not only for me but for my father, because people did not expect anything good from me as his child.

As I became older, seeing my father drunk, dirty, sleeping in the street trenches like a nobody, bloodied up from fights, I realized that he needed me, my love and care for I was all he had in the world. Therefore, I would visit him on weekends, cook, wash his clothes, clean his house, make sure he was all right and showed him love. My father's greatest delight was when I visited him, for he loved to show me off to his friends in the village center. He was so proud of what I become and could see that I was growing up into a wonderful young lady.

Eventually my father had to move to another country to start his life afresh so he could have some peace and stay out of trouble because certain people enjoyed harassing him when he was drunk to get him into trouble. Their aim was to have him in prison for life or see him dead.

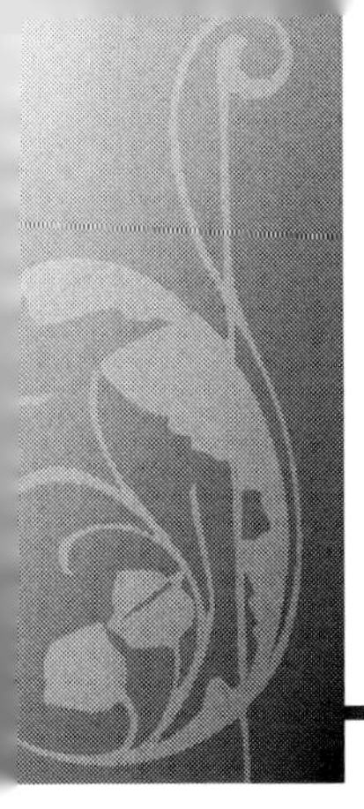

Brief Summary of Later Years

The life of a black sheep. At fourteen years old, all of my mother's family migrated to another country and left me alone in my country in the family's house, where I had to take care of myself yet again. At fifteen years, I became pregnant with my first child. I was happy because I would have someone to love me. All I wanted was love. A hurricane came and destroyed the family's house, and after a month, one of my uncles remembered me in Montserrat. He came to the island and sent me to his sister living overseas, who were capable to handle my situation, as a pregnant teenager.

The treatment I received was too terrible to mention. A week after the birth of my daughter, I was thrown out the house onto the streets with no place to live. Thus my life began again with suffering after suffering, but God is good. He always placed people in my life to help me, thanks be to God. I was homeless with my daughter on the streets, begging for food and night's rest in strangers' houses. I was evicted from apartments because I could not pay the rent. I got fired because I was smelly and dirty. I slept in an unfinished house, and the list goes on.

However, in all those situations, although it was hard, I saw God move miraculously in my life, for he always made a way for my daughter and I. Eventually I had to give my daughter to her father, one of the hardest things to do because she was my hope of being loved. I had no other choice than to give her up, in order for me to work on myself.

I'm now in my forties. My life is much better, still there is a big hole in my heart, for I never experience the love, that unbreakable bond that every little girl desires as a child, and was desperately lacking growing up and even into adulthood. However, I am grateful that God bestowed on me His love, and in return, I was able to give and show love not only to my children but also my father, for just like me, he too was searching for love and acceptance. By me being able to give him love, it makes me very happy and proud to be his daughter. I don't have my father in my life anymore, and oh, how I wish he were alive today, for he was the one person who truly loved me. And thus we gravitated from each other's love. Now he is no more, I feel so alone and unloved in this world. The Word of God is so true, for it tells us, when your mother and father forsake you, the Lord will lift us up, which is so true. The only time I experience genuine love is when I am studying and reading the Word of God. I feel peace, love, joy, and excitement, and I become so alive. That is what keep me going on day by day, grateful for the love of God. The Bible tells us that in everything we must give God thanks, and I am so grateful to God for His mercy, grace and favor on my life. If it had not been for Him, I wouldn't have been able to testify about His goodness in my life. I'm grateful he used my auntie to find me. I'm thankful for my grandmother who brought us up in church, for its the Word of God that sustained me throughout all of my ordeals, thus giving me strength in times of weakness.

The way we begin in life is not necessarily how our life will end. Therefore, no matter the problem, if we trust and hold on to God, he will see us through, "for we are more that conquerors through Him that loved us."

Printed in Great Britain
by Amazon